One Stop Notes
for G.C.S.E on:

# Dr Jekyll and Mr Hyde

by Robert Louis Stevenson

# Tasneem Raja

M.A. (Hons) English Literature

AMAZING BOOKS

*One Stop Notes on
Dr Jekyll and Mr Hyde*
Published in 2025 by
**Amazing Books**
West Wing Studios
Unit 166, The Mall
Luton, LU1 2TL
amazingbooks.uk

Text and illustrations
copyright © 2025 Tasneem Raja

*To my Mum – my strength*
*and*
*My Dad who is watching from somewhere.*

# Acknowledgements

A profoundly sincere and heartfelt Thank You to everyone who made this book possible:

Paulette Dowle

Amazing Books

My family and my friends

My students

Joseph Lyons

...and last but not least, to Mr Robert Louis Stevenson himself, *in memoriam*

# Contents

# 1: Author Biography

Full Name:      Robert Lewis Balfour Stevenson

Date of Birth:      13th November 1850

Place of Birth:      Edinburgh, Scotland

Date of Death:      3rd December 1894 (aged 44)

Place of Death:      Vailima, Upolu, Samoa

Based on Stevenson's poem *Requiem*, the following epitaph is inscribed on his tomb:

> Under the wide and starry sky
> Dig the grave and let me lie
> Glad did I live and gladly die
> And I laid me down with a will
> This be the verse you grave for me
> Here he lies where he longed to be
> Home is the sailor home from the sea
> And the hunter home from the hill

The requiem appears on the eastern side of the grave. On the western side the biblical passage of *Ruth 1:16-17* is inscribed:

> Whither thou goest, I will go;
> and where thou lodgest, I will lodge:
> And thy people shall be my people,
> and thy God shall be my God:
> Where thou diest will I die,
> and there will I be buried.

Robert Louis Stevenson was aged thirty-five when *The Strange Case of Dr Jekyll and Mr Hyde* was published in 1886.

Stevenson was born and lived in Edinburgh for most of his childhood. His father, Thomas, was a prominent engineer, well known for designing lighthouses. Most of his paternal family were engineers. His mother, Margaret, hailed from the upper class; her father was a Minister in the Church of Scotland. Both his mother and father were devout Presbyterians – *Devout* means that they were deeply religious.

He was persistently unwell as a child and spent a lot of time being tended to by his loving and equally devout nurse, Alison Cunningham affectionately known as *Cummy*. Stevenson spent many childhood holidays in his grandfather's home.

Stevenson was an only child. His frequent ill-health kept him away from school, so he was taught by private tutors. He wrote a lot of stories all throughout his childhood.

However, as Stevenson grew up, he drifted away from his conservative upbringing. He dressed in a Bohemian manner, wore a velveteen jacket and grew his hair long, all of which symbolised his rejection of the accepted social rules of behaviour at the time. He visited cheap drinking houses and brothels. Also, by the age of twenty-two, he had become an atheist, to the great distress of his parents; being an *atheist* means that he no longer believed in God.

It is said that the story for *Jekyll and Hyde* came to Stevenson in a dream, and according to his stepson, Lloyd Osbourne, he wrote the first draft of the novella in just three days. His wife, Fanny Osbourne, criticised it, after which Stevenson tossed the manuscript into the fire. Stevenson then rewrote it, taking a whole ten days this time.

The novella was published in January 1886, selling in record numbers both in the UK and in the USA.

Stevenson spent his life travelling and writing. He died in Samoa in 1894, aged just 44.

# 2: Illustration of Dr Jekyll's House

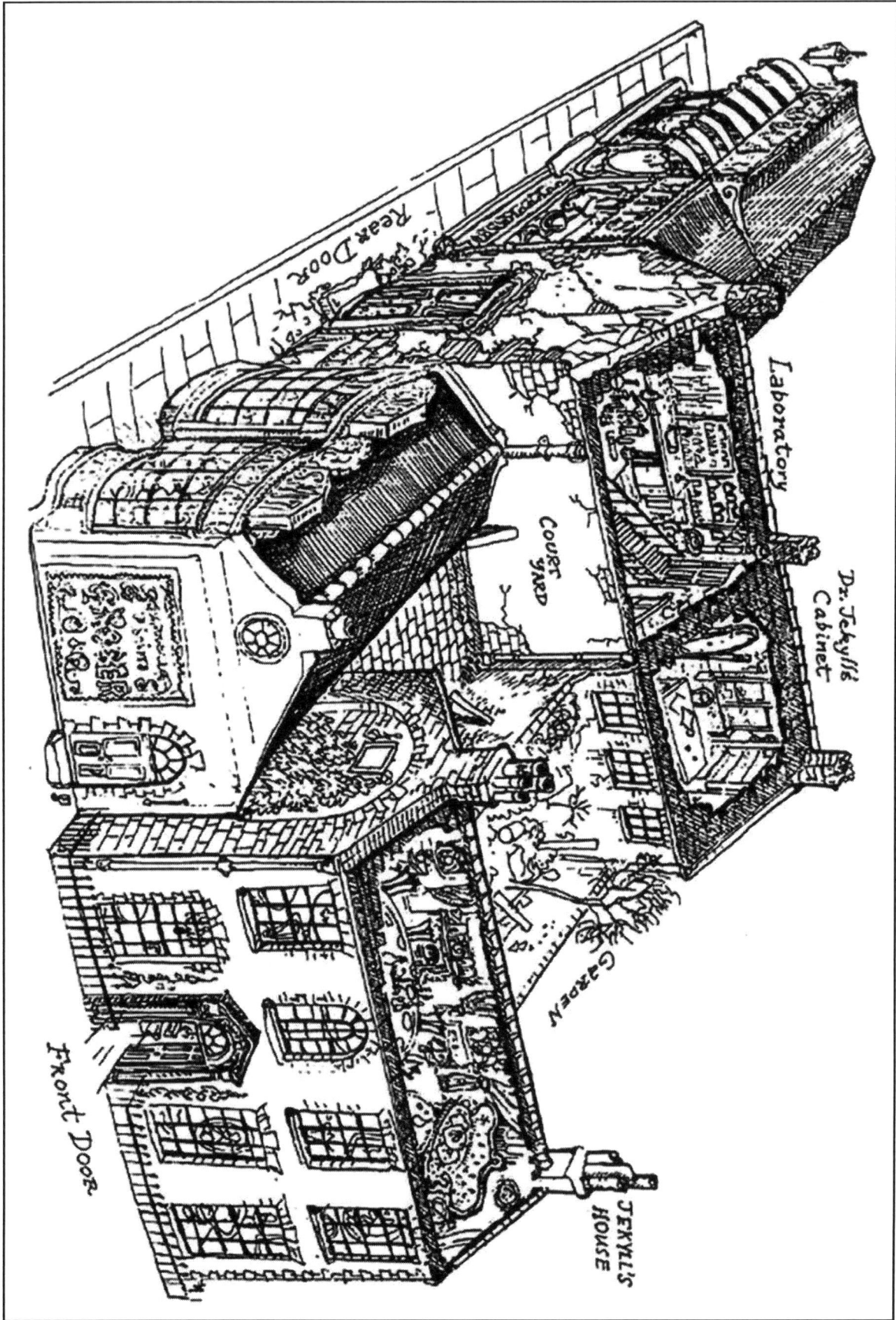

Courtesy of rghsgcseenglish.wordpress.com

# 3: Important Dates

| 1450 – | The Bethlem Royal Hospital in London was the first recorded lunatic asylum in Europe. The hospital admitted its first mentally ill patients in 1407. |
|---|---|
| 1600 –1925 approx. | British Colonial Empire. |
| 1742 –1848 | Philip Astley – a six-foot, ex-cavalry London man, is often credited as being the father of the modern circus. |
| 1760/1840 –1925 | Agricultural Revolution leading on to the Industrial Revolution, a period of huge economic and colonial growth. |
| 1764 | First Gothic novel – *The Castle of Otranto* written by Horace Walpole. |
| 1816 | *The Vampyre* by Dr John Polidori and *Frankenstein* by Mary Shelley were published. Both stories were conceived upon the same night, with *Frankenstein* also coming from a dream. |
| 1828 | Burke and Hare Murders in Scotland. |
| 1837 –1901 | Victorian Era. |
| 1850 –1894 | The life of Robert Louis Stevenson. |
| 1856 –1939 | The life of Sir Sigmund Freud. |
| 1859 | Charles Darwin's *The Origin of the Species* published. |
| 1860 | *The Woman in White* by Wilkie Collins is considered to be the first detective novel. |
| 1862 –1890 | The life of Joseph (John) Merrick, "the Elephant man". |
| 1871 | Charles Darwin's *The Descent of Man* published. |
| 1880 –1900 | *Fin de Siecle* – meaning 'end of century', a feeling of social degeneracy and moral decay versus hope and new beginnings. *Despair and hope.* |
| 1886 | *The Strange Case of Dr Jekyll and Mr Hyde* published, set in London in the same year. |
| 1887 | The 'birth' of Sherlock Holmes, in *A Study in Scarlet* by Sir Arthur Conan Doyle. |
| 1888 | The Whitechapel Murders by Jack the Ripper; five killings directly accredited to him. |
| 1897 | *Dracula* by Bram Stoker published. |
| 1920 | Freud's Essay on the *Id, Ego and Superego* published. |

# 4: Introduction

## *The Strange Case of Dr Jekyll and Mr Hyde* by Robert Louis Stevenson

The 'Strange Case of Dr Jekyll and Mr Hyde' by Robert Louis Stevenson was published, and set, in the year 1886. The novella is, at its core, a battle between good and evil. It lays out the dualistic notion that all humans are made up of two halves: the moral and the immoral, the kind and the cruel, the good and the evil, and that the one half is constantly seeking control over the other. We are all universally engaged in this interior and phenomenological (meaning, related to the self) power struggle.

Illiteracy (to not be able to read and write) was extremely high in the lower classes throughout the nineteenth century. Thus, the primary readers of fiction in 1886 were typically middle-class gentlemen. However, Stevenson's book is a scathing and brutal attack on this exact tier of society. It is a complex novella, written in code so as not to overtly insult its probable reader, while exposing that same reader to their own hypocrisies and fears.

The notable absence of middle-class women is not because all the characters are closeted or sexually repressed homosexuals, as has been suggested by some critics, but is in fact because these "ladies" are almost completely invisible in a patriarchal society. They cannot stray outside the boundaries of strict societal codes of behaviours and morality.

Powerless themselves in an unforgiving patriarchy, women needed to maintain their chastity and honour, because there was too much at stake for them to behave in any way that might smear their reputation in middle-class society and compromise their prospects of marriage. Their bodies and autonomy ( the ability to do as they pleased), were constantly policed by other men, as well as by other women.

Middle-class men, then, ruled a society, which was deeply segregated by wealth and class. They acted with impunity (meaning free from punishment), and with no fear of being held to account by any law enforcement agencies. Bear in mind, British law enforcement was in its early days and was essentially made up of low-class men, and therefore middle and upper-class men were able to use their wealth and power over police officers with ease, whether through bribery, hush money, or through making threats.

The primary theme and purpose of the novella therefore is to expose the hypocrisy of middle-class men, and to criticise a society which held itself to an unattainable standard of perfection, and compelled loose behaviour to go underground and become deviant. Hypocrisy means when you pretend to be one thing but are another.

The novella was intended to be published just before December 1885 to cash in on Christmas time. Charles Dickens had done the same in 1843 with A Christmas Carol; a tactic which proved highly profitable. However, Stevenson's wife, Fanny, insisted that he make further changes to the manuscript to get it passed the censors, since strict decency laws were in place at the time that disallowed any art or literature that could be seen as "obscene". It was eventually published in January 1886.

Stevenson hid his opinion of middle-class men in a rich vocabulary and coded lexicon where criticisms can be found in individual words and phrases. Stevenson may have been more obvious in his first draft, but the subsequent redrafting made for a much more subtle and covert narrative.

The novella should be read as though we are unaware that Jekyll and Hyde are one and the same. This is difficult to achieve since a modern audience would be aware from various films, tv adaptations and numerous references in popular culture that this is the case.

It is testament to the brilliance of the story that it still resonates today and has become part of the fabric of society. Its reference is now universal, it has become synonymous with split personalities.

It is a classic for all time.

The novella was sold as a cheap shilling shocker and sold 40,000 copies in just six months.

**Note: I have referred to middle-class gentlemen as MCM throughout these Notes, and Robert Louis Stevenson as RLS.**

# 5: The Writer's Purpose and Intention

1. To expose the hypocrisy of middle-class men – they behaved well during the day, and may have appeared decent and moral, yet by night, they were out living an immoral and evil 'other life'.

2. To do so in code, since middle-class men were the primary readership.

3. To criticize a religious and strict Victorian society that held itself to an unsustainable and impossible standard of behaviour.

4. To expose the fears of the middle classes.

# 6: Duality

**Cave Bestia – *Beware the Beast***

Darwin challenges Biblical Creationism, saying that we have a common ancestor with Apes. We have a beast in us!

← **The Beast Within Us All** →

Christianity confirms this in the form of Original Sin – it tells us to repress our wild, immoral side, and deny it, destroy it.

↓

Freud/ psychoanalysis states we have an *id* – he says that if you repress this id, your wild, feral side will find another way out – it will not just disappear.

# 7: Themes in Brief

1.  The Hypocrisy of middle-class men in Victorian society.

2.  The duality of mankind – good/evil; man/beast; us/other.

3.  What religion and society say about the evil in us all, and what RLS and Darwin say.

4.  Duality is *natural*, not *unnatural* – it is in us all of us.

5.  Hence duality is reflected and represented everywhere: London/weather/night and day/Jekyll's house.

6.  The Solidarity of MCM.

7.  Reputation of MCM – reputation is visual, external: illusion vs. reality.

8.  Reputation must be preserved – restrained, exemplary conduct.

9.  Reputation is class-based – MCM only care about *each other's* reputation. They do not care how they are seen by the lower classes.

10. Gossip destroys reputation.

11. Silence is part of the Solidarity – secrecy protects the Reputation. Hence the notes and letters – these are all about secrecy. Utterson himself keep secrets.

12. MCM are silent because they are ALL up to no good. And they know it!

13. Repression and suppression. Religion says repress your forbidden urges. Society says behave in a restrained way. However, repressing dark desires does not make them disappear. They come out in dark, violent ways.

14. Religion is primarily symbolic of hypocrisy in the book. MCM attended church and read the Bible but were still up to no good.

15. Prevalence of men – only men were up to no good.

16. Hyde is not so much as a character, as a SYMBOLIC REPRESENTATION of FEAR.

17. The rising of the lower classes – the restructuring of society.

18. Violence against innocents is a prevailing theme.

19. There is a connection between the potion and alcohol – both represent immoral uncontrolled behaviour. We drink we lose our inhibitions and control.

20. Money is power. Power enables abuse. Jekyll's money is eventually left to the single childless Utterson – foreshadowing the end of the old ways.

21. Health and sickness associated with moral corruption.

22. Scientific technology versus supernatural – reason versus immorality.

23. Man taking over God's role, usurping God through the power of science.

# 8: Context AO3 and Themes in Detail

## 1. Charles Darwin and the Theory of Evolution

- The Descent of Man was published in 1871. In this, Darwin suggested that apes and humans came from a common ancestor known as "the missing link". The missing link theory was enough to create a huge uproar in Victorian London and beyond; it shook the foundations of society.

- In the first instance, it discounted the creation story that man was descended from Adam and Eve, thus challenging Bible, God, and the entire Christian faith. At this deeply Christian time, to disprove or challenge the existence of God would have been shattering for many.

- Furthermore, Darwin's theory challenged the long-held perception that the British were inherently more civilised than other populations. One of the motivations of colonialism was that the British had a "civilising impact" on indigenous people; however, if the British themselves, like everyone else on Earth, were descended from wild beasts, then where did that leave their superiority in being refined and decent?

- This shook the Victorians to their core.

## 2. Class

- The middle classes were seen as the moral leaders of society, an image that the middle-classes constructed themselves in order to justify their entrenched social position. The novella presents the hypocrisy of this class and the notion that they presented themselves as being unwaveringly moral and upstanding. The novella details that irrespective of class, we are all capable to great depravity.

- When it comes to defining what middle-class meant at the time, we can say that the Victorian middle-class was inextricably linked to city growth and economic expansion. The popular term at the time of "the middling sort" described those between the aristocracy and the workers: a growing faction who were neither impoverished workers nor titled aristocrats. This group included businessmen, entrepreneurs, shopkeepers, and merchants involved in manufacturing and trade.

- The expansion of commerce and finance, such as banks and railways, created jobs for clerks, managers, and professionals. Economic growth, and the rapid expansion of cities across Britain, also expanded local government and the state, creating roles for civil servants, teachers, doctors, lawyers, and clerks. Therefore, some middle-class individuals amassed great wealth, while others earned modest wages. The economic boundaries were blurred, with some middle-class people becoming as wealthy as aristocrats, and some skilled workers earning as much as the lower middle-class.

- Historians have argued that the middle-class made fortunes during the early industrial revolution and used their economic success to gain political power through the 1832 Reform Act. This political power allowed them to shape policies reflecting their interests. Through education reform, civic improvements, and market growth, they believed they were providing opportunities for the working class to advance.

- However, ultimately, the middle-class were agents of capitalism, who were keen to make money above all else. There is strong evidence to suggest they had a resentment towards lower class people, and viewed their poverty as a personal failure, rather than a systemic one.

### 3. Original Sin

- Original sin, also known as ancestral sin, is the Christian view of the nature of sin, which states that sin is inherent in everyone from birth.

- Genesis 3 tells the story of how sin first entered the world. Adam and Eve were tempted by the Devil, disguised as a snake, in the Garden of Eden. They ate an apple from the Tree of Knowledge after God had forbidden them to do so. When God discovered their transgression, he banished Adam and Eve from the Garden on to the Earth.

- Evil had now come upon the world – this is known as the Fall, or the Fall of Man. It is believed that this transgression was the "original sin", and as the descendants of Adam and Eve, we all possess the innate capacity to sin and disobey God's orders.

### 4. Crime

- RLS is close-lipped on the immoral and illegal activities of Jekyll and Hyde, and indeed most of the MCM mentioned in the novella. We can be fairly sure that the immoral activities centred around sex, gambling, and drinking.

- This is a time when poor people were routinely hanged for petty theft. Many of the poor survived on prostitution. Child prostitution was rife. The legal age of consent was twelve years old, but the authorities never policed or enforced this. Gambling was also hugely commonplace.

- Male homosexuality was illegal and severely frowned upon, giving rise to the Blackmailer's charter. If a MCM was found to be engaging in homosexual acts, this opened him up to being blackmailed. In the Adventure of Charles Augustus Milverton featuring Sherlock Holmes, Sir Arthur Conan Doyle highlights how lucrative this 'profession' of blackmailing could be. Of course, only the wealthy could be blackmailed, since they had large reputations to uphold and unlike the lower classes, MCM had money.

- It is from the stories of Sherlock Holmes and Charles Dickens wherein we get a sense of Victorian London's criminal underworld, and the fraught interactions between the classes that lived within it.

- Crime is almost always directly related to poverty, and thus the desperate poverty and misery that characterised lower class existence at the time fed criminal activities and opened the door to exploitation and abuse from the higher classes. These people would do anything for money, legal or otherwise, because they were starving and desperate.

### 5. Law enforcement and the police

- The novella was written at a time when law enforcement and the police force were slowly becoming more established and powerful, being awarded authority and power through legislation.

- Police officers were typically recruited from the lower classes. We can see this class distinction when Utterson goes to see the body of Sir Danvers Carew. MCM felt they were above the law, and so to be held accountable for their actions by men of the lower orders was offensive to them and challenged their belief of their own superiority.

- Utterson does not name Dr Jekyll, seeing as it is Jekyll's stick which is the murder weapon, and he recognises it as such. Instead, Utterson immediately takes the officer to Hyde's residence in Soho.

## 6. Sex and Sexuality

- The Victorians had an extremely repressive attitude towards sex and sexuality. This was a time when any mention of sex in public spaces or in private homes was deemed to be deeply uncouth; the arts were heavily censored by law, and pornography was an underground and illicit art form. Censorship did not only apply to images but to novels and the written word as well.

- We are told very little about what MCM in the novella get up to behind closed doors, but sexual "deviancy" would certainly have been a high possibility. Since the code of honour and chastity was prevalent in the higher-class women, it followed then that the women that were available for MCM were of the lower classes.

- Elaine Showalter, a well-known feminist critic, has called the book 'a fable of *fin-de-siecle* homosexual panic, the discovery and resistance of the homosexual self' in which 'Jekyll's apparent infatuation with Hyde reflects the late nineteenth-century upper-middle class eroticisation of working-class men as the ideal homosexual objects'.

- This idea of homosexual repression and its violent effects in the novella is extremely subtle, because if RLS had been more blatant, the book would have been censored immediately.

## 7. Repression

- Sobriety, restraint, prudence, thrift, modesty, chastity, and repression were the virtues that had to be aspired to. It was assumed that the rich already practiced these virtues, and that they were rich because they deserved to be. This was the same with the poor, it was believed that they were poor because they deserved to be.

- It was considered against societal norms to exhibit unrestrained, emotional or abnormal behaviour. Freedom of expression and indulging wild, passionate behaviour was directly opposed to the Victorian mindset of repressing such desires in the name of virtue, and, through virtue, building wealth, health, and happiness.

## 8. Family

- The family unit was the most important institution in Victorian society. The home and family were sacred and had to be preserved and protected.

- In the novella, none of the men have families. However, the solidarity of the MCM amongst themselves is a substantial theme. The MCM all lived very comfortable and self-satisfied lives. They did not like change or anything that might threaten their comfort. It is worth noting that to a Victorian reader, the absence of a family unit (a wife or children) for many of these characters would have struck them as suspicious and concerning, and the reader would have thus had doubts from the outset about their morality.

## 9. Religion

- The Church of Scotland under which RLS grew up followed a version of Protestantism called Calvinism, after the preacher John Calvin (1509-1564). It called for an unwavering, totalitarian commitment to morality from both society and from within us. It called for a perfection which RLS felt was impossible to live up to and stood at odds with human nature. RLS felt the church and religion were therefore basically hypocritical.

- However, religion was a universal convention in Victorian society.

- Despite a religious revival in the early 1800s, widespread urbanisation and deepening class divides led to lessening Church attendance. In 1851, only 40% of the population were regular Churchgoers.

- By 1900, the Church was also losing its hold over the middle-classes. This would have fed upper-class anxiety at the time that those below them were becoming less religious and thus more likely to sin and commit crime. Nevertheless, Christianity had a strong influence where it held.

- All the characters in the novella demonstrate religiosity: Jekyll reads religious texts; Lanyon feels that science and God should be separate; Utterson reads "**dry divinities**" every night before he goes to bed; Hyde blasphemes in Jekyll's book.

- Jekyll's actions are shown to be sinful through religious language. For example, Jekyll is a "**secret sinner**" and Hyde is the "spirit of hell".

- Dr Jekyll and Mr Hyde symbolise good and evil, the angel and the demon. This internal struggle between two conflicting forces reflects the Biblical idea of the eternal struggle between good and evil within us all.

- In the last chapter, Jekyll confesses that his "**original evil**" emerged and took hold, referring to original sin.

- Despite RLS being an atheist, he brings to his novella a gravitas and seriousness by using religious language and allusion. By incorporating the authority of God and the Devil into his presentations of morality and immorality, the text harnesses the persisting fear in society that God sees all, and that we will be punished for our sins in the next life, by an Almighty God.

## 10. Reputation

- Preserving one's reputation was of the upmost importance at this time. Reputation, however, only operated within one's class. Individuals from lower classes had no reputation beyond their class. However, the further up you were within the class system, the bigger your reputation was, and thus the harder you needed to fight to protect it.

- MCM at this time were expected to be charitable and hold high morals, so that when these gentlemen walked out in public, they could hold their heads high, as shown through Utterson and Enfield, who undertake their regular Sunday walks. They can do so because their reputation is intact, and thus they do not need to hide their faces in shame. This can be held in contrast with Jekyll's increasing solitude, which coincides with the increasing damage to his reputation.

- **Jekyll's dilemma is not one of conscience. He enjoys being bad. His dilemma is that he does not want to 'look' bad in front of his peers.**

- It therefore follows that if his fellow middle-class society did not mind his gambling or womanising behaviour, then he would not have this internal moral conflict, nor the need to hide his actions. Society therefore compels or forces him to take his sinning underground.

- Reputation was how other middle-class men saw each other. They did not really care how they came across to the lower classes, since that opinion did not matter and held no weight among those with powerful positions in government or any other influential institution, or among the bloated aristocracy of the time; people who came from extremely wealthy and powerful families. These were the people that MCM were keen to impress.

- Reputation then is how one is viewed in the social sphere in which one resides or is directly adjacent to. One's reputation must be perfect, moral, good, with no blemishes of any kind. It reflects the importance of appearances, facades, and impeccable surfaces, which hide a dirty and sordid underside. Indeed, it's no wonder Hyde works as a double entendre, as it is a homophone of "hide". London was also full of beautiful facades on brand new buildings, and beautiful clean parks, such as Hyde Park in Central/West London, where many middle and upper-class people lived and still live today. However, London also had a dark underside of violence and immorality, a lot of which was orchestrated by the middle and upper classes.

- Reputation is also the reason why Hyde is described as physically different to Jekyll. Reputation relates to the face and the body, as these are the two things we cannot hide forever. We cannot disguise ourselves all the time. Our reputation is attached to our physical identity, hence why Jekyll's change is a physical one.

- For the Ancient Greeks, a beautiful body and face was also considered to be direct evidence of a beautiful mind and moral compass. This notion regained popularity during the Renaissance movement in Europe (1450 to 1650), and later became an entrenched idea in people's minds.

## 11. Gossip

- Gossip is the ultimate danger to reputation. Gossip can taint it and ruin it, without ever needing to be true. Gossip is the destroyer of reputation. This connects to the themes of silence and secrecy that runs throughout the novella.

## 12. Silence of the MCM

- If gossip then is harmful to the all-important reputation, then silence MUST be observed by the MCM. People had to practice silence, and repress the desire to gossip, as this code protected all of them from having their misdemeanours brought to light.

- Secret means that which is hidden from others. It is hidden because invariably, it is something bad. MCM kept each other's secrets because they all had the same secrets – their immoral, hidden behaviour.

## 13. The Hypocrisy of the Middle Classes

- At the heart of the story rests the hypocrisy of MCM.

- Hypocrisy means claiming to have higher standards or more noble beliefs than are held. When one routinely engages in the behaviours one deems and judges to be immoral.

- MCM claimed to be religious and good, as well as noble and decent. However, secretly, many of them prove to be the exact opposite. This hypocrisy also carries over to religious hypocrisy. Many of the MCM attended church regularly and read the Bible, appearing as though they are pious and morally upstanding when really, it is all just a facade.

## 14. The Duality of Man

- This leads on to man's dual nature. Through his main characters, RLS is essentially revealing that we are all comprised of good and bad. We all have a wild and feral side to our nature, that desires chaos. It is a part of us, and it is natural. However, this dark side is forced to be suppressed (by wider society) and repressed (by the self) because of social and religious codes of behaviour.

- RLS further expands on the fact that repressing our dark side is unnatural, it is like fighting nature. Therefore, in suppressing this wild side, it does not simply disappear. In fact, quite possibly, the pressure makes it contort and get worse. It is *exacerbated*.

- The issue is therefore one of CONTROL. We do not have to bury our dark sides, but we do have to control them, whilst nurturing our naturally good and moral sides. The conflict of the novella resides in the question of: which side prevails, which gets control of the other?

- Ultimately, Jekyll represents the good, and Hyde represents the bad. The good in Dr. Jekyll and the evil in Mr. Hyde are constantly trying to overpower each other to prevail and take control.

- RLS foretells what psychoanalysis would later clarify. He also references Darwin and his theories.

## 15. The Solidarity of MCM

- Many MCM at the time were living this dual life: good during the day, bad at night. Consequently, these men may have often run into each other at the same brothel, or at the same gambling house, or getting high at the same opium den.

- Since gossip destroys reputation and silence is key to preventing this, it makes sense that MCM become a united body, constantly looking out for each other. They are bolstered and united by their wealth, influence, and social circle, but they also understand the code of brotherhood, which is known to keep all transgressions, no matter how cruel or dangerous, a secret from the wider world.

- Therefore, their unity helps maintain a blanket silence amongst themselves and against anyone from the lower classes.

## 16. The Rise of the Lower Classes

- The consequences of the Industrial Revolution brought huge changes to cities like London. On the one hand, the influx of workers from the rural south saw cities being flooded by low class and impoverished people. They flocked to cities that were inadequately built to house them, leading to a rise in slum areas, such as the infamous East End, and a greater disparity between rich and poor areas.

- West London and parts of Central London were affluent or wealthy, but the East End and Soho were poor and suffered appalling conditions. Poverty and crime were high in these areas.

- By the 1850's, the Industrial Revolution was at its productive peak. However, alongside the increasing wealth of the middle classes that came with the Industrial Revolution, there was also another change occurring, as more and more people became acquainted with The Communist Manifesto, which had been published in 1848: Trade Unions.

- By the 1880s, trade unions were becoming fully legally recognised entities. This would lead to the rise of socialism and the end of the poor feeling the need to be deferential to the rich.

- British Colonialism and British Industry were also having a huge effect on the lower classes. On the one hand, the lower classes were developing a self-awareness, particularly of their own sheer numbers, which led directly to the rise of working-class consciousness, and this sewed the seeds of socialism.

- This was a class that was calling for workers' rights and respect: the basis of what Trade Unions seek to achieve. This new movement was terrifying to the middle classes who were used to being the untouchable overlords of the lower classes, without being challenged at all.

## 17. Domestic Servants as a Privileged and Privy Lower Class

- As a character, Poole is both loyal and obedient. However, it is interesting how the servants have a narrative of their own. There is a sense that the lower classes are instrumental in exposing the secrets of the higher classes, as they are privy to all the information shared amongst them in their opulent drawing rooms and at their dining tables.

- The servants represent a form of social leakage and transition, which gives rise to social mobility. The servants as carriers of the letters are connected to revealing and concealing crucial information, and thus they can expose their masters at any time. Whilst many choose not to, that power is still there. Letters and doors are both presided over by the servants.

- In The Adventure of Charles Augustus Milverton (1904) by Sir Arthur Conan Doyle, illicit love letters are leaked by the servants, since it is the servants who know all the secrets.

## 18. Colonialism

- Britain at this time was a powerful nation. It had a stable government, expanding franchise, and an expanding, advanced economy. It was also at the height of its imperial power. Despite this, over three quarters of the population were poor and low class.

- Colonialism was allowing for the rise of the "nouveau riche", or newly rich, through new investment opportunities, and the advent of new jobs, sectors, and careers, as Britain needed to maintain its influence and power in its colonies, as well as transporting and selling all the goods it transported from those colonies back to Britain.

- The comfortable middle classes were therefore shocked to see the lower classes encroaching into middle class enclaves. Strict class separation had always been rigorously maintained, as can be seen in separate parts of the houses in the novella and London itself.

- There are hints of England's Colonial project and its effects on society when a pall, the sheet that covers a coffin, is described as 'chocolate-coloured', since chocolate is not native to England. Colonialism was also helped by a rapid increase in travel and technology. During this time, the British Empire spanned over a third of the world. There was a time at which the sun was always shining on one of Britain's colonies, and therefore the empire became revered as "the empire on which the sun never sets". This was the Golden Age, and it allowed for a massive increase in trade.

- The British Army and its various factions was also a force to be reckoned with at this time, and it often resorted to violence to maintain control over native populations.

- However, back on the British Isles, people only saw the positives: the arrival of exciting new goods from all over the world undoubtedly fed a pride in being British, as many people did not recognise that much of this new wealth was earned through subjugation, exploitation and violence.

## 19. Psychoanalysis

- Freud was an Austrian neurologist and the founder of psychoanalysis, the study of the mind. Sigmund Freud was born on 6 May 1856 in the Czech Republic.

- In 1900, his major work 'The Interpretation of Dreams' was published, in which he analysed dreams in terms of unconscious desires and experiences. Then much later, in 1923, he published' The Ego and the Id', which suggested a new structural model of the mind, divided into the id, the ego, and the superego.

- This personality theory saw the human psyche structured into three parts that all developed at different stages in a person's life. Of course, all his ideas were purely hypothetical, however they were based off of years of research and therapy with real patients.

- According to Freud's theory, the id is the primitive and instinctive part of the mind that contains sexual and aggressive drives, and hidden memories. The super-ego operates as a moral conscience. Lastly, the ego is the realistic part that mediates between the desires of the id and the super-ego.

- Although each aspect of the personality has unique features, they all interact to form a whole, and each part makes an important and irreplaceable contribution to a person's behaviour.

- Jekyll and Hyde are not contextually influenced by the influence of Freud, since Freud post-dates the novella. However, we can apply Freud's theories to the book with great success.

- The establishment of insane asylums, as well as new diagnostics of and treatments for madness, became a significant part of Victorian society. In this way, Hyde could also be seen as a manifestation of Jekyll's madness.

- Mentioning psychoanalysis in reference to Jekyll and Hyde is required AO3.

## 20. Asylums

- The Victorian era saw upheavals and developments in the treatment of mental illness, marked by the construction of asylums. Victorian asylums were often large, imposing buildings, reflecting the societal fear and stigmatisation of mental illness. These institutions were typically isolated from towns and cities and set within huge grounds.

- These institutions aimed to provide care, shelter, and treatment for individuals suffering from various forms of mental illness. However, the medical community was still in its infancy in terms of knowledge and understanding, and treatments were unscientific and sometimes harmful and traumatic. It was a place of chaos and confinement. Often, the inmates were treated like animals. It was the stuff of nightmares.

- Within Victorian society, madness was a taboo subject, something to be hidden and kept secret from public view. The term "madness" covered a wide spectrum of mental health issues. Victorian literature reflected society's changing obsession and fear of mental instability.

## 21. Fin de Siècle

- The change from one century to another led to feelings of great anxiety in society at the time. The change from the 19th century to the 20th century also coincided with progressive technological and scientific advances, which further fed the fear of an unpredictable and ever-changing future.

- People were terrified of what the twentieth century would bring, rightly so, as it would bring two apocalyptic world wars within its first half.

## 22. Atavism

- In 1876 Lombroso, an Italian criminologist, proposed an atavistic form as an explanation for offending behaviour. Essentially, he focused on the idea that criminals looked bad.

- Lombroso suggested that there was a distinct biological class of people that were prone to criminality. These people exhibited 'atavistic' (i.e. primitive) features. Atavistic derives from the word "avatus", which means ancestor in Latin.

- It therefore follows that there is a genetic component that can determine the likelihood of someone being a criminal.

- These atavistic characteristics, he argued, denoted the fact that the offenders were at a more primitive stage of evolution than non-offenders; they were "genetic throwbacks". Facial characteristics indicated eyes too close together, or a low, overhanging forehead, or thick, heavy features.

- According to Lombroso, this made these individuals wild and feral and unable to fit into mainstream society, and so they would inevitably turn to crime.

- This implied that criminality was inherited and that it could be identified by physical defects. So, if you looked ugly on the outside, you were therefore ugly on the inside, reaffirming the Ancient Greek notion of beauty meaning morality.

- This Victorian obsession with looks leads to contextualisation of the freak show which saw huge prevalence at this time.

- Joseph Merrick also known as John Merrick, the Elephant Man, was born in 1862 with severe physical deformities. He was seemingly normal till the age of five, when he began to exhibit huge growths all over his body, including his face. Modern prognosis attributes him as having suffered an extremely rare case of the disease Proteus Syndrome. He was immortalised in the very unsettling but brilliant 1980 period film of the same name, directed by David Lynch and starring John Hurt as the pathetic and tragic John Merrick.

- He was called the Elephant Man because it was said that his horrendous physicality was because his mother had been trampled by an elephant. This leads us to the Victorian world of circus attractions, and notably freaks. They were called freaks but in fact, they were disabled individuals, sidelined by mainstream society and out of sheer desperation to survive, they were exhibited to the public. Many however, were exploited and abused by cruel 'owners.' It was a dark and murky world indeed.

- The 'human curiosity' movement of the nineteenth century fed the fascination and fear of the unknown and those who looked different.

## 23. Urban Terror

- London had a population of one million in 1800. By 1900, this had risen to 6.7 million, with huge numbers also coming in from Europe. It was the biggest city in the world at this time.

- Soho and the East End became hugely overpopulated, with buildings and living infrastructures unable to cope with such a vast influx of people, all of whom were desperately poor. With no sanitation and no running water, coupled with the smog of industrial areas, London becomes a vivid metaphor for rich and poor, and the effects that wealth and poverty have on morality.

- London was segregated by wealth and class from rising slum areas. This disparity also saw a rise in crime. This elevated the sense of danger around the city, with the crowd potentially hiding a sinister evil from the criminal element. Concurrent to this, large scale engineering was also underway, including the London sewage system, which was one of the finest of the time.

- The Whitechapel murders, ascribed to Jack the Ripper, began in 1888, and led people to believe that the novella had inspired the murders. Possible suspects pointed to aristocracy and royalty, and at the most probable, towards a highly educated individual. The similarities to Jekyll and Hyde are uncanny to say the least.

## 24. Opium and Drugs

- In Oscar Wilde's novel *The Picture of Dorian Gray* (1891), he wrote: "There were opium dens where one could buy oblivion, dens of horror where the memory of old sins could be destroyed by the madness of sins that were new."

- Opium was brought into the East End of London by Chinese merchants. There were no 'dens' reported beyond the East End of London, and the literature of the period overplays exactly how many existed.

- Opium was used predominantly as a medicine rather than purely for getting high.

- The Victorians of all classes suffered ill-health and for most of them, opium was an invaluable pain reliever, as well as a cure for certain illnesses. Addiction, where it existed, was seen as being more of a medical problem than a moral failing. Victorian pharmacists served everyone, and most items, including narcotics, could be purchased over the counter.

- In 1868, the Pharmacy Act recognised dangerous drugs and restricted their sale to registered chemists and pharmacists. It was not until the end of the nineteenth century, did scientists or physicians warn about the dangers of drug addiction, and legislation became more severe.

- It has been reported that RLS wrote the second version of the novella in six days under the influence of cocaine, which was a new miracle drug, prescribed to him to help alleviate the pain of his ill-health. However, there is an undeniable connection between alcohol, drugs, and their intoxicating effect on releasing humankind's dark side, as it causes people to become uninhibited and lose all sense of judgement, in the novella.

- People being drunk and violent was a particular concern of so-called Temperance Groups. Temperance means control, and these groups realised that drunken behaviour led to violence, and campaigned against the manufacture, supply and consumption of alcohol. While England never quite achieved total prohibition of alcohol like the USA, it nevertheless had active campaigns throughout the century to try to achieve it. Women were very vocal in these campaigns, since many of them were on the receiving end of the drunken violence of men, whether in a domestic setting, or out on the street.

- By the end of the 19th Century, it was estimated that about a tenth of the adult population were deliberately teetotal.

- The connection between Jekyll's potion and chemicals, releasing Hyde is clear. Drugs and alcohol are the gateway between good, rational reason and morality and the 'other' side, which is evil, irrational, wild and feral, leading to the supernatural.

- All things supernatural are connected to Demonic or Pagan Evil.


## 25. Letters and Writing

- The novella is filled with the theme of writing and letters. Communications between MCM, and even the narrative itself, are all forms of written documentation thus helping to create fear, mystery, and secrecy. There are various occasions when the narrative brings in other accounts, including epistolary forms (epistolary means letters and diary entries; items written by people first hand) which make the narrative feel more real and familiar. We call this eerie feeling of reality in a book *verisimilitude*.

- We also have the mystery of Jekyll's dual handwriting, and Dr Lanyon, who had his death warrant "written" on his face. Stevenson frames the whole novella within these items of documentation, balancing the line between myth and truth.

## 26. Mystery

- The novella is based on mystery. Mystery means that which we do not know. Mystery is also connected to Secrets. The plot maintains itself to keep from revealing that Jekyll and Hyde are in fact ONE individual until the very end. RLS probably chose to introduce Hyde to the reader before Jekyll to ensure that the reader assumes that Hyde is a completely separate entity.

- Mystery takes the senses from the real world into the surreal. When we do not know something, we delve into our imagination and within our imagination, we can conjure things darker and far more sinister than anything in the real world.

- Mystery is inherent in setting, character, plot, pathetic fallacy, the sky, letters and, in a wider sense, in the lives of MCM, who kept their mouths silent on their immoral activities. They were, quite literally, a walking mystery: they seemed knowable and trustworthy, but deep down, many of them had shocking secrets.

## 27. Violence

- Violence runs throughout the novella. Violence and the threat of it bring fear and terror.

- The novella explores the idea that violence is part and parcel of the evil that resides within all of us: evil breeds violence just as violence breeds evil. Be it physical, emotional, or psychological, violence comes out as brutality, hurt, pain, force, power, strength, ferocity, savagery, cruelty.

- When Hyde tramples over the little girl, or crushes Sir Danvers Carew, RLS presents the way that evil is inevitably revealed through violence. It is both a reaction to repression and proof of the need for repression in many instances.

- Violence is also the expectation and realisation of a threat, in a foreboding and menacing way. It is argued by many that words can also be violent, in that they can have lasting effects for years, just like physical violence.

## 28. Science and Technology

- The Victorian era accounts for some of the most exceptional advances in science and technology. From the steam engine and railways to the telegraph and the telephone, to electricity and photography, the Victorian era was an exciting and prosperous time.

- The title, Dr Jekyll's final statement: ("Here then, as I lay down the pen and proceed to seal up my confession, I bring the life of that unhappy Henry Jekyll to an end"), and Utterson's investigative activities all suggest that the novella is a scientific document. Not to mention the potion which has clear and unprecedented (meaning never seen before) transformative effects.

- Science ultimately empowers mankind to do amazing things. To the Victorian public, for whom science was only taught at a very advanced level and only for those who could afford to keep their children in school beyond the age of twelve, science was a complete mystery. Potentially, it could be perceived to be like magic or alchemy. It had power.

- Therefore, Jekyll using a scientific *lexical field* can be seen as Jekyll taking away God's power, and substituting himself as all-powerful, or omnipotent. Science is man's knowledge, knowledge that has come from intense study of God's world: and so, representing Man exposing God's secrets.

- The potion also gives power to Man to transmogrify, it takes the power away from God and enables Man to unlock the secrets of his own inner self. *Transmogrify* means to change into something abnormal and unnatural.

- By merging genres, RLS unites science and technology with the Gothic and the supernatural, thus bringing these latter two genres into the real world of facts and figures. RLS also brings in the incredibly popular sub-genre at the time, the Detective Novel, which was gaining popularity through most notably, Sherlock Holmes. Hence the novella's huge success.

## 29. Wealth

- What separates the classes is, ultimately, MONEY.

- MCM are empowered to do all they do and live the lives that they live, because they have great wealth. Wealth, which was always being topped up, and kept in the family by inheritance.

- It is wealth which separates the MCM from the lower classes and feeds their class arrogance and sense of entitlement.

- Hyde can live as he lives because he has Jekyll's wealth behind him. MCM used their wealth to get them out of trouble, and to empower their lifestyle and immoral activities. Wealth made MCM completely fearless against any authority and accountability.

- Wealth is therefore a substantial theme. It is also carried through in Jekyll's Will, which leaves everything, at the end, to Mr. Utterson.

- The physical 'copy' of the Strange Case of Dr Jekyll and Mr Hyde, like the money, is left at the end solely in the hands of Mr Utterson. He holds the narrative and the letters which expose the story, and he also holds the money. Given his reticence, his suppressed, silent, secretive nature, and his solidarity with his fellow MCM, it is likely that the 'strange case' will never see the light of day. Because even Mr Utterson feels compelled to protect the interests of his class, despite the horrors that have been committed.

- Mr Utterson has no children and apparently no family to leave his wealth to. The fact that the MCM in the novella are all unmarried heralds the eventual end of their kind—the passing of an immoral and debauched society, coinciding with the fin de siècle.

# 9: Symbols

1. **Night and day** symbolise duality, mystery and fear.

2. **London and Soho** symbolise duality, mystery and class.

3. **Dr Jekyll's house** symbolises duality.

4. **The wind and the moon** symbolise mystery and fear.

5. **Fog and clear sky** symbolise mystery and fear.

6. **The mirror** (the mirror is facing up). Mirrors symbolise truth and awareness. The primary readership are MCM. The mirror faces upwards towards the face of the reader.

7. **Keys** symbolise mystery, fear, and choice, leading to duality.

8. **The red baize door** symbolises rise of the lower classes and fear.

9. **Seals** – letters, safes, instructions as to opening letters – all symbolise secrecy and mystery.

10. **The potion and alcohol** symbolise CHOICE, CONTROL and immoral behaviour.

# 10: The Gothic Genre

Gothic literature is a genre of fiction which first became popular during the 18<sup>th</sup> century. The term 'Gothic' originates from the name of an ancient Germanic tribe (The Goths) who are thought to have contributed to the fall of the Roman Empire. They were typified as being savage and barbaric.

The term Gothic first became linked to literature with Horace Walpole's 1764 novel *The Castle of Otranto*, later subtitled *A Gothic Story*.

This term is also given to architecture. The National History Museum and the Houses of Parliament are built in this tradition. When you look up at them in the half-light, the interplay of shadows and tall structures and carvings evoke feelings of fear and terror in the watcher. The fear comes from not knowing what is hiding in the shadows. The human mind is capable of conjuring up more monsters than reality can.

Early novelists were concerned with social problems and were trying to establish the novel form. However, there came a time when the novel form was ready to explore this feeling of fear and terror and novelists experimented with how best to achieve this. Gothics novels opened the possibility of things beyond reason and the reality as we know it and delve deep into the supernatural and surreal

Gothic novels have key characteristics, as follows:

## 1. Setting – London, Jekyll's House, the Door

A forbidding setting is key to Gothic literature. A Gothic novel always features old castles, desolate mansions, haunted and abandoned houses and ruined buildings. These eerie settings evoke fear and terror in the character as well as in the reader.

The architectural features of the buildings such as pointed towers, trapdoors, mysterious corridors and doors, rusty hinges, and secret tunnels, all symbolise entrapment and secrecy and mystery. The settings are symbolic of evil, sin, and immortality.

## 2. Atmosphere – Pathetic Fallacy, Weather

Atmospheres of darkness and fog and mist dominate Gothic literature. The night is the key motif in Gothic novels. The darkness of night restrains the ability to see clearly and creates an atmosphere of uncertainty and powerlessness, where a character does not know what lies ahead. The plot of Gothic novels also consists of mysterious happenings, where we are kept from knowing the full story. Mystery means the unknown, and fear comes from the unknown.

## 3. The Supernatural – Hyde

Another key element of Gothic literature is its presentation of supernatural forces in the form of ghosts, vampires, giants, monsters and demons. Supernatural elements are typically evil, and where there is reference to Christianity, then these elements hail from the Devil and from Hell. There is often an 'other'; an evil character with links to the supernatural. Someone who is outside the norm of societal rules and expectations, and who behaves contrary to these societal norms. This outsider creates terror and fear in the reader. This can also be seen in the appearance of a doppelganger – a double or an alter ego. A double walker is a twin, a shadow, a mirror image.

Ann B Tracy, a critic writes that the Gothic novel can be seen to describe a fallen world. This is reflected in the concept of Fin de Siecle.

## 4. High Emotions

Gothic novels contain melodrama. Characters scream, cry, are afraid, angry, and faint. The fear of the unknown intensifies their emotions. They are always in a state of panic and sometimes suffer from the inner torments. Events like murder arouse a profound sense of emotional expression in the characters. Heightened emotions convey a feeling of fear and chaos and unpredictability. They force characters to behave in a way outside of societal norms which is terrifying.

## 5. Protagonist as Anti-Hero – Jekyll

The protagonist is an anti-hero. He is the focus of the story, yet at same time he has monstrous elements to his personality. He is an isolated and outcast person. Sometimes, we see the protagonist carrying the burden of guilt and suffering from inner torments. He is doomed, meaning destined to fail, and gradually moves towards his ultimate decay and death.

## 6. Women as Victims – the Fainting Maid/the Girl that Hyde Trampled/the Women Who Wanted to Get at Hyde at the Beginning

In Gothic fiction, women are seen as victims. The fear and threat of the powerful and, in many cases, of the unknown make them scream, cry and faint. Sometimes their suffering also results from some sort of illness or guilt or their helplessness at the expense of a powerful male. This emphasises the severity of the threat and the violence; it presents perspective and contrast. Violence in a battle is watered down and expected but violence against the weak and vulnerable is reprehensible.

## 7. Curses and Omens – the Immorality of the Rich, Money Being a Curse, Jekyll Feeling the Curse of Hyde

Portents (ill omens), curses and prophecies play a major role in Gothic literature. They are deliberately embedded into the plot to foreshadow terrible events. The past of the characters is usually haunting their present. For example, a son has to pay for the sins of his father. The protagonist of the Gothic story suffers either from a familial curse or an old prophecy.

## 8. Dreams and Nightmares – Utterson's Dream/MCM, Their Fears and Their Immoral, Hypocritical Behaviour

Gothic literature appeals to the subconscious by way of fear. Nightmares, visions and alcohol/drug-induced hallucinations expose the characters' deep-rooted fears and guilt of past sins. The repressed past of the characters reappears in the form of visions and nightmares. These nightmares and visions also reveal to the reader the characters' hidden fears.

## 9. Frightening Sounds – Danvers' murder/the Breaking of Bones

The creaking of the door, the monstrous laughter of some unknown creature, the mysterious sound of footsteps. All these sounds help convey a frightening tone. These sounds also create an atmosphere of eeriness, suspense, and mystery in the Gothic story.

## 10. Weather

Fog in Gothic stories enhance the atmosphere of suspense and terror. The fog particularly signifies the obscurity of objects. It reduced visibility and hides the truth.

## 11. Religion – Christianity

The faiths typically see human beings as sinful. The church has lost its supremacy. The monks and priests are represented as the perpetrators of violence. As faith retreats, horrors and fears take its place. No supreme power is there to save the victims of Gothic horror. God has been abandoned. The Gothic world reveals a new world, a fallen world, in which fallen men live in fear and alienation.

## 12. Psychology – Jekyll and Hyde

The inner fears and psychological instability of the self is another key element of Gothic fiction. The characters' guilt of past sins or preoccupation with the realms of the unknown render them either psychologically unstable or mentally ill. Their inner fears and unforgivable transgressions constantly haunt them. Finally, the characters' psychological trauma ultimately leads to their split personality, and they become a threat for the surrounding people.

## 13. Good Versus Evil

Initially we find the protagonist as the embodiment of evil but gradually his suppressed goodness overcomes the apparent evil side of his character. In some texts, we see that the character is torn between the good and evil and ultimately ends up being grey; neither completely good or evil.

# 11: Religious References and Definitions

| Cain's Heresy | In the Bible, the sons of Adam and Eve were called Cain and Abel. Both brothers offered a sacrifice to God and God favoured Abel's sacrifice. One day, Cain killed Abel and hid his body. When God asked Cain, 'Where is your brother?' Cain famously replied, 'I am not my brother's keeper'. |
|---|---|
| | Heresy is the same as blasphemy which means that which is against God. |
| | Cain is also seen as evil and Abel as good. |
| Israeli Tabernacle | *"For any drug that so potently controlled and shook the very fortress of identity, might, by the least scruple of an overdose or at the least in opportunity in the moment of exhibition, utterly blot out that immaterial tabernacle which I looked to it to change."* |
| | This is a reference to the Israeli tabernacle, which was said to house God. Jekyll uses it to refer to his body and soul. |
| Captives at Philippi | *"The drug had no discriminating action; it was neither diabolical nor divine; it but shook the doors of the prisonhouse of my disposition; and like the captives of Philippi, that which stood within ran forth."* |
| | After the Battle of Philippi in 42 BC, the victors, Antony and Octavius, released the captives. The captives were those who had supported Brutus and Cassius (the defeated), Julius Caesar's assassins. |
| | Hyde, freed from his prison goes on to murder Sir Danvers Carew. |
| The Babylonian Finger | *"This inexplicable incident... seemed, like the Babylonian finger on the wall, to be spelling out the letters of my judgment".* |
| | King Belshazzar was a Chaldean King. Because he did not bow to the Israeli (Judeo-Christian) God, a ghostly hand appeared and wrote out his death sentence on a wall with his finger. |
| | The kingdom was invaded that night. Jekyll alludes to this Biblical scene because it explains his mental state of conflict, and how he has set himself up against God. It foreshadows Jekyll's death and evokes a feeling of doom. |

# 12: Mr Edward Hyde

...one a little man who was stumping along eastward at a good walk

It wasn't like a man; it was like some damned Juggernaut.

"He is not easy to describe. There is something wrong with his appearance; something displeasing, something down-right detestable. I never saw a man I so disliked, and yet I scarce know why. He must be deformed somewhere; he gives a strong feeling of deformity, although I couldn't specify the point. He's an extraordinary looking man, and yet I really can name nothing out of the way."

He was small and very plainly dressed and the look of him, even at that distance, went somehow strongly against the watcher's inclination.

Mr. Hyde was pale and dwarfish, he gave an impression of deformity without any nameable malformation, he had a displeasing smile, he had borne himself to the lawyer with a sort of murderous mixture of timidity and boldness, and he spoke with a husky, whispering and somewhat broken voice;

There is something more, if I could find a name for it. God bless me, the man seems hardly human! Something troglodytic, shall we say.

> *And next moment, with ape-like fury, he was trampling his victim under foot and hailing down a storm of blows,*
>
> *Particularly small and particularly wicked-looking, is what the maid calls him," said the officer.*
>
> *"Quite so, sir," returned Poole. "Well, when that masked thing like a monkey jumped from among the chemicals and whipped into the cabinet, it went down my spine like ice."*
>
> *"…my master, and there's the truth. My master"—here he looked round him and began to whisper—"is a tall, fine build of a man, and this was more of a dwarf."*

Hyde is not so much a character as a symbolic representation of FEAR. FEAR comes from the following:

- Threats to one's security.
- The supernatural – the devil, monsters, evil.
- Mystery, the unknown, secrets.

His physical description is vague and all that can be said of him is that he is *small and dark*.

He is rarely seen alone – always in the presence of a good character to provide contrast. He has no narrative of his own. We see him reflected through the perceptions of others. This is why he is different things to different people.

1. To the lower classes – he is the EVIL inherent in the exploitative, oppressing abuse suffered by the lower classes at the hands of MCM – the violence, the rapes, the abuse – he is pure inhuman cruelty – hence the reaction of the women in chapter 1 who wanted to get at him.

2. To the Sawbones, the low-class doctor who would be witnessing the consequences of the actions of MCM – the underage pregnancies, the botched abortions, the suicide attempts, Hyde represents EVIL, which is why he had such a bad reaction to Hyde.

3. To the comfortable middle classes, he is the embodiment of all their FEARS, which is why he brings out the terrors in Enfeld, Utterson and Dr. Lanyon.

To the Middle-classes, Hyde represents the 'Damned Juggernaut' that is:

1. The rising of the lower classes – He is short; has a defiantly criminal nature and lives in an unrespectable area. This is how the MCM viewed the lower classes.

2. To them, this rising movement is an unholy and unstoppable force.

3. Hyde represents secrets – the MCM hid their nighttime/immoral activities. In this way he shows them as mysterious. They hid their immoral activities, kept them unknown, did not reveal or speak of them.

4. Hyde also means hide as in outer skin – he therefore represents reputation.

5. Hyde is pure evil – the more you indulge the less it can be controlled. He is the wild and feral part that is a part of all of us – see psychoanalysis.

6. He is the exploitative and abusive aspect of the MCM – violent, malevolent, evil and cruel.

Industrialization and Colonialisation were essentially restructuring society and the social hierarchy, making diverse men rich – the nouveau riche were moving into wealthy areas thus threatening the security of upper-class strongholds – to them, this was monstrous and a damnation. It was malevolent and evil.

This was a society which operated on POWER AND CONTROL. The rich have power and used it to their advantage, abusing and exploiting the weak lower classes. Hyde represents a challenge to this power, which is why Lanyon, Utterson and Enfield react in a repulsed and horrified way.

# 13: Synopsis

The action takes place over some eighteen months: One Sunday in November → that same evening → two weeks later → one year later in October → two months Dr Jekyll returns to old self → end of January Dr Lanyon dies → last night takes place in March.

## Chapter 1 – The Story of the Door

Every/most Sundays, Mr Gabriel John Utterson of Gaunt Street and his distant cousin Mr Richard Enfield take their typical walk together in silence.

On this particular Sunday afternoon, in November 18_ , they walk past a door and Mr Enfield recounts a story about it, which occurred a few weeks earlier. He witnessed a child being attacked by a sinister looking man. He collared the man who agreed to pay one hundred pound as compensation to the girl's family who had quickly gathered around. He took them to this particular door and entered using a key. He returned with ten pounds in gold and a cheque. Enfield tells Utterson that the man's name was EDWARD HYDE and the name on the cheque was well known. They waited overnight with the man, in Mr Enfield's chambers, Hyde took them to the bank and the cheque was cashed forthwith.

Enfield says that he thought it smelled of blackmail and that he had seen Hyde enter/exit many times, in fact, he saw him do so a week ago.

Utterson hints that he knows the other man.

## Chapter 2 – The Search for Hyde

That SAME evening, Utterson goes to his business room after dinner and takes out Jekyll's Will which states that in the event of the death or disappearance of Dr Jekyll after 3 months, some three quarters of a million pounds goes to Hyde.

That SAME evening, Utterson goes to his business room after dinner and takes out Jekyll's Will which states that in the event of the death or disappearance of Dr Jekyll after 3 months, some three quarters of a million pounds goes to Hyde.

Utterson decides to go see Dr Hastie Lanyon who lives on Cavendish Square. Dr Lanyon tells him that he has not seen Jekyll for over ten years, and he has not heard of Hyde. Utterson returns home; after a nightmarish sleep, he decides to wait and see Hyde near the door. He waits for an undisclosed number of nights. At last, one night around 10, he is successful. He meets Hyde, who gives him an address in Soho. Utterson, disturbed by the meeting, goes around the corner to Jekyll's house. Poole the butler says he is out. Poole is aware of Hyde and states that all the servants have been given orders to obey Hyde. Utterson returns home.

## Chapter 3 – Dr Jekyll Was Quite at Ease

TWO WEEKS LATER. Dr Jekyll gives a dinner party. He denounces Lanyon. The two talk about Hyde. Dr Jekyll presses Utterson to secure Hyde his rights in terms of the will to which Utterson reluctantly agrees.

## Chapter 4 – The Carew Murder Case

(TWO MONTHS before the murder, Jekyll changes into Hyde without the use of the potion – this is taken from his statement at the end.)

NEARLY A YEAR after Jekyll's dinner party in chapter 3, on this night in October, a maidservant witnesses the murder of Sir Danvers Carew. Danvers carried a letter addressed to Utterson and Hyde carried a stick that Utterson had once given to Jekyll.

She sees the murder at 11 pm, faints, and comes round at 2 am when she reports the murder. Half the stick is left at the scene.

The police visit Utterson next morning. He identifies the body and takes the police to Soho. The housekeeper admits to having seen Hyde less than an hour ago. His room is ransacked. He had come after almost TWO months. Utterson and the police go to the bank where several thousands of pounds are in Hyde's account. He however, has gone missing.

### Chapter 5 – Incident of the Letter

THAT SAME AFTERNOON, Utterson goes to see Jekyll. Poole shows him to the dissecting rooms at the end. Jekyll is aware of the murder and distraught. He claims that Hyde has gone and shows Utterson a letter from Hyde. He said that he burned the envelope, and that it had been delivered a short while ago.

Utterson asks Poole if any letter came for Jekyll that day, and is told no. He returns home and sits with Mr Guest, his clerk who also happens to be a handwriting expert. He compares it to a letter from Jekyll and deciphers the two hands as one. Utterson privately believes that Jekyll is covering up a murderer in Hyde.

### Chapter 6 – Incident of Dr Lanyon

Time passes. Reports of Hyde's nefarious activities are heard. For two months, Jekyll returns to his old self. On the:

*8th January* – Utterson, Jekyll and Lanyon dine as old friends at Dr Jekyll's house.

*9th January* – Jekyll writes to Lanyon who takes the compound from Jekyll's house and sees Hyde change to Jekyll.

*12th, 14th and 15th January* – Utterson visits Dr Jekyll but is not admitted.

*5th night after that dinner party, the 16th January* – Utterson dines with Mr. Guest.

*6th night, so the 17th January* – Utterson goes to Dr Lanyon's house.

He is admitted but Dr Lanyon looks awful; he says that he has had a shock and names Dr Jekyll as the cause. Utterson returns home and writes to Dr Jekyll asking what has happened.

The following day he receives a reply saying that the quarrel is irreparable, and that Jekyll now needs to be left alone.

A Week later, 25th January, Dr Lanyon takes to his bed and less than another week later, Dr Lanyon is dead.

The night after the funeral, Utterson returns to his business room. He opens a letter from Dr Lanyon, for Utterson's eyes only; and, in the event of Utterson's predecease, the letter and its contents are to be destroyed.

Utterson opens the seal to reveal another letter; to only be opened in the event of the disappearance or death of Dr Jekyll.

Utterson's honour as a lawyer prevents him opening it.

Utterson calls on Jekyll but at each call, is told by Poole that he is either asleep or confined to his laboratory. Utterson visits less and less.

\*

## Chapter 7 – Incident at the Window

Another Sunday walk, a few weeks later, Utterson with Enfield. They pass the door again and Enfield relates that he has since found out that the door is at the back of Jekyll's house. They decide to step into the court where they see Dr Jekyll sitting in the middle window looking sad. They all talk when suddenly, a look of terror freezes on Jekyll's face and he slams the window down.

Utterson and Enfield silently and in shock walk away.

## Chapter 8 – The Last Night

March. Utterson sits by the fire one evening when he receives a visit from Poole. He offers the distraught Poole a drink. Poole tells him that something bad has happened to his master. They both leave and Utterson is pleased to note that the wine is untasted.

They go to Jekyll's house where the hysterical servants admit them. They take a candle and Poole knocks on the Cabinet (laboratory) door. The voice within is different. Poole that whatever is in the room has killed his master. The voice changed eight days ago. It has been crying for some medicine that cannot be got hold off. Poole explains that Jekyll often wrote him notes and threw them on the stairs for Poole to get. Utterson asks sharply "how did you come by this note." Poole replies that the chemist returned it. Utterson reads that Jekyll has been trying to get hold of some salt, but that the old lot was impure and cannot be got more of.

Poole explains that he saw 'it' in the theatre at the end of the garden one day – it was looking for something, digging amongst the crates. When it saw Poole, it ran back to the Cabinet. Poole claims it was wearing a mask.

They set Bradshaw the footman to guard the exits.

Poole and Utterson stand by the door and hear the creature inside; they break down the door to find the twitching body of Hyde on the floor, wearing Jekyll's clothes.

They search for Jekyll but cannot find him. The find the key to the back door, on the floor, broken and rust covered.

They return to the cabinet, where they see a mirror facing up towards the ceiling. Upon the table, is a large envelope containing several enclosures. There is a new Will with Hyde's name replaced with Utterson's name; a letter from Jekyll dated that same day, instructing Utterson that he has disappeared and to first read Dr Lanyon's sealed letter, and then his own unhappy confession. This is in a third enclosure that was entrusted to Poole who now hands this to Utterson. It is now 10 at night. Utterson says that he will return at midnight, and they will then inform the police.

## Chapter 9 – Dr Lanyon's Narrative

Dr Lanyon writes this letter to Utterson on the 9th January, 4 days after the incident with Hyde.

He received the letter from Jekyll in the evening, telling him that he is to go to Jekyll's house that night, where Poole will let him in, he is to bring a drawer of chemicals and wait back at his house till midnight.

There is a PS, that if the letter is not delivered, to enact these wishes the next day.

Lanyon sets out and is admitted. There is a carpenter and a locksmith waiting there. Lanyon takes the chemicals and returns to his house. At midnight there is a knock on the door. Lanyon admits Hyde. Hyde is dressed in oversized, rich clothing.

He asks Lanyon for a graduated glass and proceeds to mix some chemicals. He drinks.

Dr Lanyon is the only person to ever witness the change from Hyde into Jekyll. It is only at the very end of the novella; do we realise that JEKYLL IS HYDE and vice versa.

## Chapter 10 – Henry Jekyll's Full Statement of the Case

Jekyll writes in the first person.

He is born into a wealthy family. Grows up tall, handsome and accomplished. However, he loves being good, but he also loves being bad. The only problem is that he wants to be SEEN as good all the time. He does not want his reputation to suffer. He still wants to hold his head high. He realises that man can be split into two and he turns to the laboratory table for help. He does not tell the ingredients of his potion because it was incomplete. One of the salts had an impurity; he had purchased this wholesale.

One night, he takes the mix. The change is painful, a kind of birth. As Hyde he glories in his evil. There was no mirror at the time, but he had one brought in later so he could witness his change. He drinks again, and changes back to Jekyll. Jekyll is aware that he is getting old, and his immoral life was not at ease with this fact. He therefore releases Hyde. He took up rooms in Soho, gave orders to his servants to obey Hyde, and wrote up the Will.

He begins his new life. He refers to the accident with the child and the meeting with Enfield.

Two months before the murder of Danvers, Jekyll returns home as himself, goes to bed, and wakes up as Hyde! He is alarmed, runs downstairs, and remembers then that the servants have been told to admit him.

Hyde can go and get the potion and turn back into Jekyll. He is afraid that Hyde is becoming more powerful. While Jekyll is aware of what Hyde gets up to, Hyde does not care what Jekyll gets up to.

Jekyll decides he will forego Hyde and commit to Jekyll. However, he succumbs to temptation, takes the compound and changes. It is at this point that he murders Sir Danvers Carew.

He realises the next day that it has been put out that Hyde is the murderer. He can no longer let Hyde out because he will be captured and put in prison or hung.

One day in January, sitting on a bench in Regent's Park, he faints and when he comes to, he has changed into Hyde. He cannot go home, and he cannot be seen. He thinks to ask Lanyon for help. He takes a hansom to a hotel where he waits in a private room. He writes the letter to Dr Lanyon. Hyde is resisting Jekyll. On his way to Lanyon's, he strikes a matchgirl in the face.

At Dr Lanyon's he changes back.

Jekyll is now turning into Hyde at regular intervals and is having to take double doses to maintain himself as Jekyll. He now needs the potion to revert back to Jekyll. Hyde is appearing without the potion.

That was a week ago. The statement ends with Jekyll in conflict. It seems that he had enough control to finally kill Hyde. At the final blow at the door, Jekyll takes cyanide at the precise point that he turned into Hyde.

Utterson has all the letters, the statement and the Will in his possession at his house.

*

# 14: Narrative Technique

The novella employs a complex narrative technique. It has TEN chapters; the final chapter is dedicated to Dr Jekyll's first-person narrative, written in the last hours and days of his life. It is Dr Jekyll's confession. It is found on the table alongside the amended Will.

The central mystery in the novella rests on the fact that Jekyll and Hyde are two separate individuals. This mystery is only resolved at the very end of chapter 9, which is Dr Lanyon's letter to Utterson, written in the last days of his life, and held in Utterson's safe until the stipulations or conditions upon it are finally realised.

Aside from these two letters, the novella is written in the third person, with the primary focus on Utterson. We the reader, only know what he knows.

Utterson is an excellent narrator. He has been given a silent and serious personality so as not to steal the thunder from the central characters of Jekyll and Hyde. His purpose in the novella is to propel the plot forward. It is also to conceal, since we share his ignorance as well as his knowledge, as well as his fears and solidarities.

We know from Dr Lanyon, that Dr Lanyon and Dr Jekyll parted ways some ten years ago. We also know that Dr Jekyll handed Mr Utterson his Will some time before, but we are not told when exactly. It is clearly since the inception of Hyde.

The action from when we first meet Mr Enfield and Utterson on their Sunday morning walk at the beginning of the novella, to Utterson breaking in Jekyll's cabinet door, spans some eighteen months. Jekyll has been working towards the potion for some ten years. He bulk-bought the impure salt, so he has been Hyde for as long as the impure salt lasted; we do not know how long Hyde has been in existence, so to speak.

Narratives are provided in the form of statements, both verbal and written and most of the events are conveyed to readers through conversations between the characters rather than through direct witness.

The final chapter, Jekyll's statement, has been written over the previous week, because he says 'about a week has passed and I am finishing this statement under the influence of the old powders.' The statement is written in the first person from Jekyll's perspective, but at the last, there is one use of direct address, and it is likely aimed towards Utterson, when he writes, 'You will learn from Poole how I have had London ransacked…'.

While we never actually hear directly from Hyde, it is only in Jekyll's final statement do we get the dual narrative, switching between 'I' and 'he', from the perspective of Hyde, when he changes for the first time without the potion and needs Lanyon's help to change back. It is the only time we hear from Hyde.

Conflict and tension arise from the desire for power and control. Jekyll has suffered under a feeling of fatalism since Hyde has gained control.

Stevenson uses these multiple perspectives to make the reader feel powerless; as though they are an outsider looking in on the action; this intensifies feelings of horror and terror and the reader is anxious to read on, in a state of permanent suspense. It permeates the novella with an overriding sense of fear throughout.

Mention of Narrative Technique in a concise form is required in any essay. It is a structural device, alongside setting, characterisation and plot structure.

# 15: Plot Structure

The plot structure of the novella is chronological.

The central mystery in the novella rests on the fact that Jekyll and Hyde are two separate individuals. This mystery is only resolved at the very end of chapter 9, which is Dr Lanyon's letter to Utterson, written in the last days of his life, and held in Utterson's safe until the stipulations or conditions upon it are finally realised.

Aside from these two letters, the novella is written in the third person, with the primary focus on Utterson. We the reader, only know what he knows.

Utterson is an excellent narrator. He has been given a silent and serious personality so as not to steal the thunder from the central characters of Jekyll and Hyde. His purpose in the novella is to propel the plot forward. It is also to conceal, since we share his ignorance as well as his knowledge, as well as his fears and solidarities. Ironically, through his own characteristics as a MCM does he inadvertently help maintain the mystery; for example, when the body of Danvers Carew is discovered, Utterson sees the stick, knows it belongs to Dr Jekyll, but takes the police to Hyde's residence in Soho.

The plot is propelled forward in the form of statements, both verbal and written and most of the events are conveyed to readers through conversations between the characters rather than through direct witness.

# 16: Answering Technique

You may notice that almost all questions in English Literature, begin with the word 'How?'

- How does the writer show...
- How is this presented...
- How far do you agree...

Most schools have an acronym for how to answer this question. Usually this is a form of PEEL – **point**, **evidence**, **explanation**, **link**. However, many students find that this doesn't help them answer questions as fully as an examiner is looking for.

In this book, we will use a different acronym that will help you answer such questions in the best possible way. The acronym we will use is:

## DEQALT – MC

Let's talk about **DEQALT – MC**. The letters stand for:

**D**: Device     **E**: Example     **Q**: Question     **A**: Analysis     **L**: Link     **T**: Themes

→     **M**: Mood     **C**: Context

Using this acronym, you can answer each question with the following structure:

RLS uses – name the **Device** – quote an **Example** – link it to the **Question** – **Analyse** the device – **Link** it to other **Themes** – add **Mood** – finish with **Context**.

Your essay will therefore be a series of DEQALT MC paragraphs.

Let us look at the Device in more detail. Exam boards require use of technical language. So you need to name the device, which will be one of the following:

- Setting
- Plot points – what they reveal.
- Narrative Technique – point of view
- Characterisation – gender, class, age.
- Language devices – nouns, verbs, adverbs, adjectives, grammar, punctuation.
- Figurative Language devices – similes, metaphors, personification.
- Irony
- Themes such as evil and duality.

Now for an example.

**Question:**

How does Stevenson present the theme of evil in this extract?

> *"And next moment, with ape-like fury, he was trampling his victim under foot and hailing down a storm of blows, under which the bones were audibly shattered and the body jumped upon the roadway. At the horror of these sights and sounds, the maid fainted."*

**Answer:**

Evil means extremely immoral, wicked and cruel – to have no goodness whatsoever. Stevenson uses the adjective 'ape-like' to present evil. Ape-like denotes savagery, animalistic rage and strength and feral wildness. This represents the nature of our universal, innate duality that it is uncontrollable and evil. We all carry the seeds for this within us. This conveys a mood of terror and fear. At the time, Darwin had presented his studies which connected man and ape as having one ancestor. Given that the Victorians were mostly Christian and considered themselves civilised, this challenged their belief in God as well as challenged all that they believed themselves to be.

Let's break our answer down into **DEQALT–MC**

Evil means extremely immoral, wicked and cruel. To have no goodness whatsoever. Stevenson uses the adjective 'ape-like' to present evil. (AO1)

**D**: Here we *name the device* - in this case we have chosen a **language device** from the list on the previous page.

**E**: We also *quote an Example*, i.e. **'ape-like'**.

**Q**: We *link our device* to the question, i.e. **'to present evil'**.

Ape-like denotes savagery, animalistic rage and strength and feral wildness. (AO2)

**A**: We break down the **definition** of 'ape-like', thus *analysing it*.

This represents the nature of our universal, innate duality, that it is uncontrollable and evil. We all carry the seeds for this within us. (AO2)

**L & T**: Here we *link to other themes*: we link the **theme of evil** to the **theme of duality**, and the **unchangeable nature** of our internal animal selves.

This conveys a mood of terror and fear. (AO2)

**M**: We *detail the mood* conveyed by this device.

At the time, Darwin had presented his studies which connected man and ape as having one ancestor. Given that the Victorians were mostly Christian and considered themselves civilised, this challenged their belief in God as well as challenged all that they believed themselves to be. (AO3)

**C**: We have *added context*, considering what was occuring at the time in history the book was published.

# 17: Sample Essay

Read the following extract from Chapter 1 and then answer the question that follows. In this extract Mr Enfield tells Mr Utterson about his meeting with Mr Hyde.

> *"Did you ever remark that door?" he asked; and when his companion had replied in the affirmative. "It is connected in my mind," added he, "with a very odd story."*
>
> *"Indeed?" said Mr. Utterson, with a slight change of voice, "and what was that?"*
>
> *"Well, it was this way," returned Mr. Enfield: "I was coming home from some place at the end of the world, about three o'clock of a black winter morning, and my way lay through a part of town where there was literally nothing to be seen but lamps. Street after street and all the folks asleep-— street after street, all lighted up as if for a procession and all as empty as a church--till at last I got into that state of mind when a man listens and listens and begins to long for the sight of a policeman. All at once, I saw two figures: one a little man who was stumping along eastward at a good walk, and the other a girl of maybe eight or ten who was running as hard as she was able down a cross street. Well, sir, the two ran into one another naturally enough at the corner; and then came the horrible part of the thing; for the man trampled calmly over the child's body and left her screaming on the ground. It sounds nothing to hear, but it was hellish to see. It wasn't like a man; it was like some damned Juggernaut. I gave a few halloa, took to my heels, collared my gentleman, and brought him back to where there was already quite a group about the screaming child. He was perfectly cool and made no resistance, but gave me one look, so ugly that it brought out the sweat on me like running.*

Starting with this extract, how does Stevenson present Mr Hyde as a frightening outsider?

Write about:
- how Stevenson presents Mr Hyde in this extract.
- how Stevenson presents Mr Hyde in the novella as a whole.

**Our Answer:**

The "Strange Case of Dr Jekyll and Mr Hyde,", was written and set in 1885 and published in January 1886, Victorian London. In the chapter two extract as well as the rest of the novella, Stevenson presents Mr Hyde as a frightening outsider through his behaviour and appearance. In addition, Stevenson employs religious imagery to highlight Mr Hyde's evil and Satanic ways, thereby representing Mr Hyde as a shock to the traditional mores of Victorian society.

Stevenson uses the verb 'snarl' to present Hyde as a frightening outsider. Snarl connotes a wild and feral action; it presents danger and hostility and violence and threat. This unusual and discomforting behaviour contrasts with what a normal person would do, which is to warmly welcome a guest into their home.

Stevenson uses the simile `like a mad man` to describe Mr Hyde as a frightening outsider. Madness conveys rage, unpredictable and chaotic behaviour, someone that cannot be reasoned with, violence, threat and fear. Both snarl and mad also denote the theme of duality, that we are all like this and that it is natural and universal. In Victorian times, mental health was a taboo issue. Madness is uncontrollable, which is the anathema of a controlled, intellectual Victorian society.

Stevenson uses the adjectives, `pale and dwarfish`, to describe Hyde as a frightening outsider. This use of sensory language presents Mr Hyde to be the opposite of what a traditional Victorian man would look like: tall, strong and healthy like Mr Hyde's `polar twin` Dr Jekyll. Such an appearance would frighten Victorian people, because it was far outside the norm.

Stevenson uses the noun `deformity, 'to show Hyde as a frightening outsider. Deformity denotes people who are abnormal, unpleasant and terrifying to look at. People with such deformities, such as the Elephant Man, would be seen in shows for entertainment and shock value. In other parts of the novel, Stevenson describes Mr Hyde by saying that there is something `wrong with his appearance,` which is 'displeasing' and `downright detestable.` This use of alliteration in `downright detestable` not only brings emphasis to Hyde's appearance, but it also vividly highlights Hyde's evil and fear-inducing characteristics. Since no physical deformity is ever named, one could suggest that Hyde is more an effect that he has on others rather than a person. This relates to Hyde being different things to different elements of society. To the working classes, he represents the violent abuse that the MCM inflict on them. To the middle classes, Hyde represents the evil that is the rising of the lower classes.

Furthermore, Mr Hyde is also described as being `troglodytic` or primitive, thus relating Mr Hyde to savage cavemen. Only a few decades before Stevenson's book, Darwin produced his theory of evolution. This theory states that we all evolved from one common ancestor: the primitive Ape. Victorian society, at the time, was religious and too traditional to hear Darwin's radical theory. That is why Mr Hyde's appearance is so shocking and frightening, because he embodies primitivism. In a sense, Mr Hyde's behaviour and appearance could be considered an extended metaphor of the novel that evil and savagery lies within all of us, as it does with Dr Jekyll in the form of Mr Hyde.

Finally, Stevenson employs religious and Satanic imagery to present Mr Hyde as a frightening outsider. Stevenson accomplishes this by describing Hyde as having `Satan's signature` upon his face. It's almost as if Mr Hyde has made a deal with the devil and as Satan's puppet. This metaphor is effective in painting Hyde's evil. It also raises the idea of religious hypocrisy. Stevenson was an atheist, but he saw that middle class men went to church but then still engaged in immoral activities.

Furthermore, Stevenson uses the simile `like a damned Juggernaut` to describe Hyde, suggesting that Hyde is a strong and powerful force that is condemned by God. A Juggernaut originates from the Pagan Hindu faith and also represents a powerful, unstoppable force. The thought of a powerful juggernaut would have scared a Victorian audience, because it steps into the realm of the occult and supernatural. To the middle classes, he is the horror that is the rising of the lower classes and to the lower classes he is the evil that middle class men commit upon them.

Ultimately, Stevenson writes the novella in code, so as not to offend his middle-class male readership, whilst exposing their own hypocrisy.

Indicative content Examiners are encouraged to reward any valid interpretations. Answers might, however, include some of the following:

» **AO1**
  - Mr Hyde's behaviour and reactions to Utterson
  - Utterson's behaviour and reactions to Mr Hyde
  - Utterson's shock and confusion
  - Utterson's attempt to understand his fear of Mr Hyde

» **AO2**
  - Use and effect of particular word choices to describe Mr Hyde's physical appearance and behaviour
  - Use and effect of particular word choices to describe Utterson's reactions to Mr Hyde
  - Effects of mention of 'Satan'
  - Utterson's reactions
  - Utterson's use of questions
  - Silence and solidarity of MCM.

» **AO3**
  - The ways in which social attitudes towards behaviour might impact upon what is frightening
  - Social attitudes/acceptability, illustrated with 'common friends' etc.
  - Impact of evolutionary ideas on way Hyde is described
  - Ideas about primitive nature within man: 'troglodytic' etc
  - The relationship between the text and the gothic genre

# 18: Annotated Complete Novella

## 1: Story of the Door

Mr. Utterson the lawyer was a man of a rugged countenance that was never lighted by a smile; cold, scanty and embarrassed in discourse; backward in sentiment; lean, long, dusty, dreary and yet somehow lovable.

---

Restrained behaviour, not very talkative unemotional. The solidarity of MCM – only they found him lovable. He keeps himself to himself. Repressed. Secretive.

Gabriel – the archangel of Anunciation – to announce something; to make a statement.

John – the revealer of the secrets of the godhead – meaning truth, and morality.

We are assured that Utterson is a credible narrator, but he is nevertheless a MCM also. He too represents the hypocrisy of MCM.

---

At friendly meetings, and when the wine was to his taste, something eminently human beaconed from his eye; something indeed which never found its way into his talk, but which spoke not only in these silent symbols of the after-dinner face, but more often and loudly in the acts of his life.

---

Alcohol releasing inhibitions. We all have a repressed 'other'.

'Eminently' – very, extremely.

'Beacon' – means light, set to warn or expose.

Alcohol promotes uninhibited behaviour.

The silence of MCM, they do not talk about what they get up to.

---

He was austere with himself; drank gin when he was alone, to mortify a taste for vintages; and though he enjoyed the theatre, had not crossed the doors of one for twenty years.

---

'Mortify' means to suppress, repress. This shows that MCM CAN control their inner urges. They just choose not to. They **choose** to indulge and release their desires. It also introduces repression as a theme. It also means that Utterson denies himself worldly pleasures in keeping with societal norms of the time. To do things to excess was seen as against the strict moral code that the MCM perceived to live by.

'Gin' and 'vintages' – duality.

---

But he had an approved tolerance for others; sometimes wondering, almost with envy, at the high pressure of spirits involved in their misdeeds; and in any extremity inclined to help rather than to reprove.

> 'Envy' – wanting to emulate. The others referenced here are fellow MCM. The solidarity of MCM. They do not tell each other off, they keep each other's secrets. They are all up to no good.
>
> Another connection to alcohol and immorality – 'high pressure of spirits'.

"I incline to Cain's heresy," he used to say quaintly: "I let my brother go to the devil in his own way."

> In the Bible, the sons of Adam and Eve were called Cain and Abel. Both brothers offered a sacrifice to God and God favoured Abel's sacrifice. One day, Cain killed Abel and hid his body. When God asked Cain, 'Where is your brother?' Cain famously replied, 'I am not my brother's keeper'. To mind your own business is therefore an immoral act. Heresy is the same as blasphemy which means that which is against God. Therefore, Utterson leans towards that which is against God – he is not a moral man. It is ungodly to mind your own business.
>
> Cain is also seen as evil and Abel as good. This implies that evil is intrinsic to human nature and has been with us since the dawn of time – duality.

In this character, it was frequently his fortune to be the last reputable acquaintance and the last good influence in the lives of downgoing men. And to such as these, so long as they came about his chambers, he never marked a shade of change in his demeanour.

> Mr Utterson is a MCM. His clients will not be from the lower class, they will be his peers. His demeanour never changes because he never disapproves of the actions of his peers. He does not disapprove because he too is like them, and he has an affinity and solidarity with them. He will stand by his friends to the very end, no matter what crimes or acts they have committed, and he will continue to be on their side.

No doubt the feat was easy to Mr. Utterson; for he was undemonstrative at the best, and even his friendship seemed to be founded in a similar catholicity of good-nature.

> Catholicity if capitalized means the character of being in conformity with a Catholic church; if uncapitalised, then it means to have a liberality of sentiments or views – it is a word which in itself presents duality of meaning and therefore the theme of duality.
>
> Undemonstrative – does not show emotion.
>
> It can be seen to be an oxymoron in itself – strict and liberal at the same time.
>
> However, this means that Utterson relishes his friendships, and they also reciprocate – the solidarity of the MCM.

It is the mark of a modest man to accept his friendly circle ready-made from the hands of opportunity; and that was the lawyer's way. His friends were those of his own blood or those whom he had known the longest; his affections, like ivy, were the growth of time, they implied no aptness in the object.

> Meaning that he does not choose his friends but becomes attached to people who are around for a long time – solidarity.

Hence, no doubt the bond that united him to Mr. Richard Enfield, his distant kinsman, the well-known man about town. It was a nut to crack for many, what these two could see in each other, or what subject they could find in common. It was reported by those who encountered them in their Sunday walks, that they said nothing, looked singularly dull and would hail with obvious relief the appearance of a friend.

> 'the well-known man about town' – a euphemism for knows the night life well, up to no good.
>
> 'said nothing' – silence preserves reputation as talking is gossip and gossip destroys reputation.
>
> They complement each other. Where Mr Enfield is gregarious and boisterous; Mr Utterson is silent and a listener rather than a talker.

For all that, the two men put the greatest store by these excursions, counted them the chief jewel of each week, and not only set aside occasions of pleasure, but even resisted the calls of business, that they might enjoy them uninterrupted.

> Solidarity and silence and the strength therein.

It chanced on one of these rambles that their way led them down a by-street in a busy quarter of London. The street was small and what is called quiet, but it drove a thriving trade on the weekdays.

> Duality in the words 'quiet' and 'thriving.'
>
> London is seen as having two sides; wealthy areas just streets away from rough areas – duality.

The inhabitants were all doing well, it seemed and all emulously hoping to do better still, and laying out the surplus of their grains in coquetry; so that the shop fronts stood along that thoroughfare with an air of invitation, like rows of smiling saleswomen.

> The shop fronts are a metaphor for prostitutes. Coquetry means flirtatious behaviour.
>
> 'Emulously' means to emulate – to copy or aspire to be like; competitively.
>
> Coded language for prostitutes flaunting their wares. Poor women who were desperate for money would do anything to please.

Even on Sunday, when it veiled its more florid charms and lay comparatively empty of passage, the street shone out in contrast to its dingy neighbourhood, like a fire in a forest; and with its freshly painted shutters, well-polished brasses, and general cleanliness and gaiety of note, instantly caught and pleased the eye of the passenger.

> Any reference to religion refers to the theme of religious hypocrisy – Sunday is the day for going to church.
>
> 'Veil' – is a cover, concealment, the unknown and mystery.
>
> 'Florid' – later Dr Lanyon is described as red faced – florid and red-faced mean the same thing – therefore connecting MCM with immoral behaviour.
>
> 'Fire' means lust and passion and forest means hidden, concealed, secret.
>
> The street referred to is the main road where Jekyll lives.

Two doors from one corner, on the left hand going east the line was broken by the entry of a court; and just at that point a certain sinister block of building thrust forward its gable on the street. It was two storeys high; showed no window, nothing but a door on the lower storey and a blind forehead of discoloured wall on the upper; and bore in every feature, the marks of prolonged and sordid negligence.

> The sinister door is around the corner from the busy street from where Jekyll lives.
>
> Metaphor for Man's Duality – sinister, blind forehead, sordid negligence, all represent the evil, uncivilised, wild and feral side of man's psyche.
>
> 'Sinister' – evil, malevolent, threat.
>
> 'Discoloured' – stained, impure, corrupt.

The door, which was equipped with neither bell nor knocker, was blistered and distained. Tramps slouched into the recess and struck matches on the panels; children kept shop upon the steps; the schoolboy had tried his knife on the mouldings; and for close on a generation, no one had appeared to drive away these random visitors or to repair their ravages.

> 'Blistered and distained' – sick, ill, diseased, immoral.
>
> The door is also a contrast of meaning; so, the noun 'door' means opening and welcoming, but this door shows neglect and is unwelcoming. The nature of evil.

Mr. Enfield and the lawyer were on the other side of the by-street; but when they came abreast of the entry, the former lifted up his cane and pointed.

"Did you ever remark that door?" he asked; and when his companion had replied in the affirmative, "It is connected in my mind," added he, "with a very odd story."

"Indeed?" said Mr. Utterson, with a slight change of voice, "and what was that?"

> 'with a slight change of voice' – Utterson is uncomfortable at the sign of impending gossip. Utterson repeats this change later when discussing the Will with Jekyll and Jekyll raises the topic of Dr Lanyon.
>
> This also changes the mood to an unsettled one, as a reader, we are expecting something strange or sinister to happen.

"Well, it was this way," returned Mr. Enfield: "I was coming home from some place at the end of the world, about three o'clock of a black winter morning, and my way lay through a part of town where there was literally nothing to be seen but lamps.

> 'Some place' – unknown, mysterious.
>
> 'At the end of the world' – mysterious, hidden, obscure.
>
> '3 o clock' – up to no good, it is an unnatural time to be out and about. All good things are asleep at night.
>
> 'Black, winter' – cold and dark, man's immoral, feral side.
>
> 'Lamps' – truth, awareness, light fighting through the darkness.

Street after street and all the folks asleep—street after street, all lighted up as if for a procession and all as empty as a church—till at last I got into that state of mind when a man listens and listens and begins to long for the sight of a policeman.

> Repetition of 'street after street', highlights the extent of man's evil nature. It is currently defying the light of truth. The evil is such that it evokes fear and a desire to see any law enforcement officer for protection. 'Law and lamps' symbolise accountability. The MCM are acting without fear, partly because they are not being held to account.
>
> 'as empty as a church' – simile meaning Godless, abandonment of faith.

All at once, I saw two figures: one a little man who was stumping along eastward at a good walk, and the other a girl of maybe eight or ten who was running as hard as she was able down a cross street.

> There is no good in being out at 3 am on a black winter's morning. The little girl is probably out because she is sadly, a prostitute making money so that she and her family can eat. Enfield is also out; he's most likely visiting brothels or gambling dens or even may have just visited the little girl! MCM went out at night to commit immoral acts. There is no concept of underage sex or consent. It may legally be aged 12 at this time, but no one was checking.
>
> 'Stumping' – has multiple meanings. It means a puzzle or something confusing and perplexing. A stump is also something from which a part has been cut off, referencing duality.

Well, sir, the two ran into one another naturally enough at the corner; and then came the horrible part of the thing; for the man trampled calmly over the child's body and left her screaming on the ground.

> 'The two ran into each other naturally enough' – symbolises the violence with which MCM abuse and exploit the weak and vulnerable lower classes. It is 'natural' to Enfield.
>
> 'Trampled calmly' – oxymoron, violence with control. Control comes from power and power enables abuse.
>
> It is also an example of RLS restrained and formal language to describe a horrific event. Contrast this to the graphic language used to describe the murder of Danvers Carew.

It sounds nothing to hear, but it was hellish to see.

> Her screams mean nothing hence they do not register; but Hyde is hellish because to Enfield he represents the fear that is the rising of the lower classes.

It wasn't like a man; it was like some damned Juggernaut.

> Hyde is not so much a man as a symbolic representation. Here, we see Hyde through Enfield's perspective. 'Damned' means going to Hell, demonic; and 'Juggernaut' is a pagan, Hindu word that means an unstoppable force.

I gave a few halloa, took to my heels, collared my gentleman, and brought him back to where there was already quite a group about the screaming child. He was perfectly cool and made no resistance, but gave me one look, so ugly that it brought out the sweat on me like running. The people who had turned out were the girl's own family; and pretty soon, the doctor, for whom she had been sent put in his appearance. Well, the child was not much the worse, more frightened, according to the sawbones; and there you might have supposed would be an end to it. But there was one curious circumstance. I had taken a loathing to my gentleman at first sight.

> Interesting repetition of 'my gentleman' – Enfield uses the personal pronoun to take ownership of Hyde. This is because Hyde is a part of Enfield.
>
> Sawbones is a low-class doctor – see chapter on Hyde.

So had the child's family, which was only natural. But the doctor's case was what struck me. He was the usual cut and dry apothecary, of no particular age and colour, with a strong Edinburgh accent and about as emotional as a bagpipe. Well, sir, he was like the rest of us; every time he looked at my prisoner, I saw that sawbones turn sick and white with the desire to kill him.

> Class is so important in this novella. Just as Utterson is a lawyer for the rich, doctors too have classes. Sawbones is slang for a low-class medic, one who serves the lower classes. He would see the consequences of the actions of MCM, the underage pregnancies, the bruising, the beatings, the botched abortions.
>
> The rich do not abuse and exploit their own. They abuse and exploit the poor. They do not care about the poor. The poor have no voice and no importance, and poverty forces them to do desperate things.

I knew what was in his mind, just as he knew what was in mine; and killing being out of the question, we did the next best. We told the man we could and would make such a scandal out of this as should make his name stink from one end of London to the other.

> The MCM do not fear the law, but they fear for their reputation and their name. Remember, the low-class men and women have no reputation since they have no money.
>
> Scandal is to do with reputation and gossip. Scandal is what happens when gossip exposes the truth and destroys reputation.
>
> 'killing...next best' – Enfield equates loss of reputation with death showing just how valuable reputation is and what it means to the MCM.

If he had any friends or any credit, we undertook that he should lose them.

> Enfield threatens Hyde with the loss of his reputation and friends – both are associated with money.

And all the time, as we were pitching it in red hot, we were keeping the women off him as best we could for they were as wild as harpies. I never saw a circle of such hateful faces; and there was the man in the middle, with a kind of black sneering coolness—frightened too, I could see that—but carrying it off, sir, really like Satan.

> The women are low-class women. In Greek mythology, harpies were winged monsters with women's faces who avenged wrong doings. This shows the effect that Mr Hyde had on the women, to make them behave in such an aggressive way in response to his action. MCM abused low class women, not women of their own class.
>
> Sneering and frightened – duality in his power/evil and his vulnerability. Hyde being frightened shows that he is not all-powerful, he can be hurt or beaten.

'If you choose to make capital out of this accident,' said he, 'I am naturally helpless. No gentleman but wishes to avoid a scene,' says he. 'Name your figure.'

Well, we screwed him up to a hundred for the child's family; he would have clearly liked to stick out; but there was something about the lot of us that meant mischief, and at last he struck. The next thing was to get the money; and where do you think he carried us but to that place with the door?—whipped out a key, went in, and presently came back with the matter of ten pounds in gold and a cheque for the balance on Coutts's, drawn payable to bearer and signed with a name that I can't mention, though it's one of the points of my story, but it was a name at least very well known and often printed.

Interestingly, the wealth that enables and empowers the MCM is also what they use when blackmailed to get them out of the consequences of their behaviour.

Enfield does not mention the name on the cheque – secrecy and silence and solidarity and gossip and reputation.

Mr Enfield's attempts to get compensation for the girl do not clarify the situation, they instead deepen the mystery. This is because it is very strange that Mr Hyde could walk into a cellar door and come out with a cheque that will give him £100 when presented to the bank and in the name of Dr Jekyll. We are left wondering as to the connection is between the two men.

Note how 'well known' is repeated – it was earlier used to describe Enfield.

Coutt's is a famous bank used by the very wealthy, showing how rich the cheque owner is.

The figure was stiff; but the signature was good for more than that if it was only genuine. I took the liberty of pointing out to my gentleman that the whole business looked apocryphal, and that a man does not, in real life, walk into a cellar door at four in the morning and come out with another man's cheque for close upon a hundred pounds.

Apocrypha are Biblical or related writings not forming part of the accepted canon of Scripture because they are of doubtful authorship or authenticity. Apocryphal means things widely thought of as true but are in fact false – so MCM are widely thought of as being respectable and moral but in fact are living two lives, a nighttime one and a daytime one – a good one and a bad one.

The' goodness of one man' is challenged by the wickedness of another.

But he was quite easy and sneering. 'Set your mind at rest,' says he, 'I will stay with you till the banks open and cash the cheque myself.' So we all set off, the doctor, and the child's father, and our friend and myself, and passed the rest of the night in my chambers; and next day, when we had breakfasted, went in a body to the bank. I gave in the cheque myself, and said I had every reason to believe it was a forgery. Not a bit of it. The cheque was genuine."

"Tut-tut!" said Mr. Utterson.

"I see you feel as I do," said Mr. Enfield. "Yes, it's a bad story. For my man was a fellow that nobody could have to do with, a really damnable man; and the person that drew the cheque is the very pink of the proprieties, celebrated too, and (what makes it worse) one of your fellows who do what they call good.

> 'our friend' – ownership and familiarity with Hyde because he is in all of us.
>
> Contrast between Jekyll and Hyde. Notice the use of 'who do what they call good.' – it's non-committal and references surface and reality/ illusion and reality which means duality.
>
> 'Sneering' – contempt, scorn, looking down upon, feeling of arrogant. Low and high, inverted, because Hyde is 'low' and he is looking down on them.

Blackmail, I suppose; an honest man paying through the nose for some of the capers of his youth. Black Mail House is what I call the place with the door, in consequence. Though even that, you know, is far from explaining all," he added, and with the words fell into a vein of musing.

> Blackmail was common at this time, as well as being illegal. You can only be blackmailed if you have done something wrong not if you are innocent or 'honest'. Blackmail was lucrative since reputation was so important and MCM were all doing bad things. When they were discovered, they were threatened with exposure if they did not pay money over.

From this he was recalled by Mr. Utterson asking rather suddenly: "And you don't know if the drawer of the cheque lives there?"

"A likely place, isn't it?" returned Mr. Enfield. "But I happen to have noticed his address; he lives in some square or other."

"And you never asked about the—place with the door?" said Mr. Utterson.

> Enfield using secrecy to veil the fact that the bearer does live on this street. Note the lack of details.

"No, sir; I had a delicacy," was the reply. "I feel very strongly about putting questions; it partakes too much of the style of the day of judgment. You start a question, and it's like starting a stone. You sit quietly on the top of a hill; and away the stone goes, starting others; and presently some bland old bird (the last you would have thought of) is knocked on the head in his own back garden and the family have to change their name. No sir, I make it a rule of mine: the more it looks like Queer Street, the less I ask."

'Day of judgment' – accountability, you will be judged on your misdeeds.

'Starting a stone' – loss of control over the situation.

In many ways, Jekyll has started his own stone.

'Bland old bird' – portraying the MCM as appearing as though they are boring and staid, but that is all on the outside, the reality is much different.

The family have to change their name because of scandal – a good name comes from reputation.

'Queer Street' – blackmail usually happened if it transpired that the MCM was homosexual, since this was both illegal and scandalous. He could be blackmailed for being gay. In Sherlock Holmes, Charles Augustus Milverton is one such blackmailer who comes to a sticky end when one of his previous female victims shoots him.

"A very good rule, too," said the lawyer.

"But I have studied the place for myself," continued Mr. Enfield. "It seems scarcely a house. There is no other door, and nobody goes in or out of that one but, once in a great while, the gentleman of my adventure. There are three windows looking on the court on the first floor; none below; the windows are always shut but they're clean. And then there is a chimney which is generally smoking; so somebody must live there. And yet it's not so sure; for the buildings are so packed together about the court, that it's hard to say where one ends and another begins."

Enfield is describing the side/back of Jekyll's house; this is a clear metaphor for the duality of man. We later see Jekyll sit at the middle window when he changes.

The pair walked on again for a while in silence; and then "Enfield," said Mr. Utterson, "that's a good rule of yours."

The fact that Utterson repeatedly mentions the silence rule emphasises its importance. Silence is a protection for these MCM in so many ways. They do not speak about the things they do, they do not spread gossip. It is all to protect themselves and their reputations.

"Yes, I think it is," returned Enfield.

"But for all that," continued the lawyer, "there's one point I want to ask. I want to ask the name of that man who walked over the child."

"Well," said Mr. Enfield, "I can't see what harm it would do. It was a man of the name of Hyde."

Notice how Enfield is happy to mention the name of Hyde but not of Jekyll. Jekyll must be protected. Hyde is not one of them (so to speak), so he can be outed.

"Hm," said Mr. Utterson. "What sort of a man is he to see?"

"He is not easy to describe. There is something wrong with his appearance; something displeasing, something down-right detestable. I never saw a man I so disliked, and yet I scarce know why. He must be deformed somewhere; he gives a strong feeling of deformity, although I couldn't specify the point. He's an extraordinary looking man, and yet I really can name nothing out of the way.

> It is an odd description with no detail provided. It supports the view that Hyde is not so much a person but more the personification of concepts – a symbolic representation.

No, sir; I can make no hand of it; I can't describe him. And it's not want of memory; for I declare I can see him this moment."

> 'I can see him this moment' – Enfield is looking at Utterson. Hyde resides inside all the MCM, Utterson included.

Mr. Utterson again walked some way in silence and obviously under a weight of consideration. "You are sure he used a key?" he inquired at last.

> A 'Key' represents autonomy, choice, freedom, secrets, hidden, access, restriction, all of which are themes in the novella.

"My dear sir..." began Enfield, surprised out of himself.

"Yes, I know," said Utterson; "I know it must seem strange. The fact is, if I do not ask you the name of the other party, it is because I know it already. You see, Richard, your tale has gone home. If you have been inexact in any point you had better correct it."

"I think you might have warned me," returned the other with a touch of sullenness. "But I have been pedantically exact, as you call it. The fellow had a key; and what's more, he has it still. I saw him use it not a week ago."

> 'Pedantically' is repeated later when Jekyll calls Dr Lanyon a hide bound pedant. Pedantically means to be concerned with trivial matters while leaving main matters aside.
>
> 'Sullenness' – Enfield is sullen because he is embarrassed. He is embarrassed because he has broken the code of silence.

Mr. Utterson sighed deeply but said never a word; and the young man presently resumed. "Here is another lesson to say nothing," said he. "I am ashamed of my long tongue. Let us make a bargain never to refer to this again."

"With all my heart," said the lawyer. "I shake hands on that, Richard."

> 'I am ashamed of my long tongue' – all that has taken place, amounts to gossip. Gossip destroys reputation. MCM love their reputations and consider these to be a commodity – reputation is associated with wealth since the poor do not have reputations.

## 2: Search for Mr. Hyde

That evening Mr. Utterson came home to his bachelor house in sombre spirits and sat down to dinner without relish. It was his custom of a Sunday, when this meal was over, to sit close by the fire, a volume of some dry divinity on his reading desk, until the clock of the neighbouring church rang out the hour of twelve, when he would go soberly and gratefully to bed.

> 'Dry divinity' – alliteration. Dry meaning empty, boring, tedious, uninspiring – a curious way to describe religion. The MCM treat religion as not something they believe in but as something they do out of habit.
>
> 'Soberly' – a reference to alcohol and immorality.

On this night however, as soon as the cloth was taken away, he took up a candle and went into his business room. There he opened his safe, took from the most private part of it a document endorsed on the envelope as Dr. Jekyll's Will and sat down with a clouded brow to study its contents. The will was holograph, for Mr. Utterson though he took charge of it now that it was made, had refused to lend the least assistance in the making of it; it provided not only that, in case of the decease of Henry Jekyll, M.D., D.C.L., L.L.D., F.R.S., etc., all his possessions were to pass into the hands of his "friend and benefactor Edward Hyde," but that in case of Dr. Jekyll's "disappearance or unexplained absence for any period exceeding three calendar months," the said Edward Hyde should step into the said Henry Jekyll's shoes without further delay and free from any burthen or obligation beyond the payment of a few small sums to the members of the doctor's household.

> 'Holograph' means a will written by the named individual to whom the will relates to so basically Jekyll wrote his own Will.
>
> Money is a massive theme in this novella. It connects the ability and entitlement of the MCM to commit their immoral deeds.
>
> Notice how in providing this information, Stevenson merely emphasises the mysterious relationship between Jekyll and Hyde. Mystery means not knowing.

This document had long been the lawyer's eyesore. It offended him both as a lawyer and as a lover of the sane and customary sides of life, to whom the fanciful was the immodest.

> Utterson regards the 'fanciful' as the 'immodest' because he is conservative, who wishes only to tread the paths which are 'customary', but Lanyon uses the same word 'fanciful' to say Jekyll is being unrealistic. The rational and reasonable Utterson is offended by the unusual Will.
>
> 'Fanciful' means imaginary, phantastic,
>
> 'Immodest' also means lacking humility or decency; immoral, loose behavior.

And hitherto it was his ignorance of Mr. Hyde that had swelled his indignation; now, by a sudden turn, it was his knowledge. It was already bad enough when the name was but a name of which he could learn no more. It was worse when it began to be clothed upon with detestable attributes; and out of the shifting, insubstantial mists that had so long baffled his eye, there leaped up the sudden, definite presentment of a fiend.

> 'Fiend' – demonic, evil.
>
> Utterson is also baffled and is none the wiser. Mystery brings with it a mood of fear.

"I thought it was madness," he said, as he replaced the obnoxious paper in the safe, "and now I begin to fear it is disgrace."

> Jekyll has no descendants. All the MCM in the novella seem to be bachelors, unmarried and without families. Money enables their abusive and exploitative behaviour, so it is crucial that Jekyll keep hold of his money. The Will also anticipates that Jekyll may either need Hyde's permanent body at some point or he may already be feeling the effects of the conflict between Jekyll and Hyde. The struggle for control is already going on.

With that he blew out his candle, put on a greatcoat, and set forth in the direction of Cavendish Square, that citadel of medicine, where his friend, the great Dr. Lanyon, had his house and received his crowding patients. "If anyone knows, it will be Lanyon," he had thought.

> Cavendish Square leads Harley Street – it is a real location, lending a sense of realism to the novella and thus making the fear greater because it is real.
>
> 'greatcoat' – reputation is a cover.
>
> 'citadel' – fortress.

The solemn butler knew and welcomed him; he was subjected to no stage of delay but ushered direct from the door to the dining-room where Dr. Lanyon sat alone over his wine. This was a hearty, healthy, dapper, red-faced gentleman, with a shock of hair prematurely white, and a boisterous and decided manner. At sight of Mr. Utterson, he sprang up from his chair and welcomed him with both hands. The geniality, as was the way of the man, was somewhat theatrical to the eye; but it reposed on genuine feeling. For these two were old friends, old mates both at school and college, both thorough respectors of themselves and of each other, and what does not always follow, men who thoroughly enjoyed each other's company.

> Lanyon seems to represent the self-satisfied certainties of Victorian England: he appears to be someone who thinks he knows it all. Someone who does not like to have his reality challenged. The MCM are comfortable, why shouldn't they be? They are rich, powerful – life is good for them.
>
> MCM were very friendly with each other.
>
> 'Prematurely' white – premature means early; it links to the theme of primal and so to man's duality. It is repeated later when used to describe twilight.

After a little rambling talk, the lawyer led up to the subject which so disagreeably preoccupied his mind.

"I suppose, Lanyon," said he, "you and I must be the two oldest friends that Henry Jekyll has?"

"I wish the friends were younger," chuckled Dr. Lanyon. "But I suppose we are. And what of that? I see little of him now."

"Indeed?" said Utterson. "I thought you had a bond of common interest."

"We had," was the reply. "But it is more than ten years since Henry Jekyll became too fanciful for me. He began to go wrong, wrong in mind; and though of course I continue to take an interest in him for old sake's sake, as they say, I see and I have seen devilish little of the man. Such unscientific balderdash," added the doctor, flushing suddenly purple, "would have estranged Damon and Pythias."

> Damon and Pythias (Greek mythology): two inseparable friends. When Pythias was sentenced to death by Dionysius, Damon offered to take his place. Neither wanted to live if it meant that the other perished.
>
> 'Fanciful' – Dr Lanyon cannot see beyond his safe and comfortable world. In fact, we can see from his high emotion exactly how intolerable this is. Lanyon does not believe that Jekyll's new direction is scientific at all. This brings tension because the reader senses something sinister in the unconventional direction that Jekyll was heading.

This little spirit of temper was somewhat of a relief to Mr. Utterson. "They have only differed on some point of science," he thought; and being a man of no scientific passions (except in the matter of conveyancing), he even added: "It is nothing worse than that!" He gave his friend a few seconds to recover his composure, and then approached the question he had come to put. "Did you ever come across a *protégé* of his—one Hyde?" he asked.

"Hyde?" repeated Lanyon. "No. Never heard of him. Since my time."

> 'Protégé' means dependant, ward, disciple, understudy.

That was the amount of information that the lawyer carried back with him to the great, dark bed on which he tossed to and fro, until the small hours of the morning began to grow large. It was a night of little ease to his toiling mind, toiling in mere darkness and besieged by questions.

> 'toiling' – really working hard and only coming up with more questions and no answers – mystery.
>
> Besieged connotes the language of conflict, violence.

Six o'clock struck on the bells of the church that was so conveniently near to Mr. Utterson's dwelling, and still he was digging at the problem. Hitherto it had touched him on the intellectual side alone; but now his imagination also was engaged, or rather enslaved; and as he lay and tossed in the gross darkness of the night and the curtained room, Mr. Enfield's tale went by before his mind in a scroll of lighted pictures. He would be aware of the great field of lamps of a nocturnal city; then of the figure of a man walking swiftly; then of a child running from the doctor's; and then these met, and that human Juggernaut trod the child down and passed on regardless of her screams. Or else he would see a room in a rich house, where his friend lay asleep, dreaming and smiling at his dreams; and then the door of that room would be opened, the curtains of the bed plucked apart, the sleeper recalled, and lo! there would stand by his side a figure to whom power was given, and even at that dead hour, he must rise and do its bidding. The figure in these two phases haunted the lawyer all night; and if at any time he dozed over, it was but to see it glide more stealthily through sleeping houses, or move the more swiftly and still the more swiftly, even to dizziness, through wider labyrinths of lamplighted city, and at every street corner crush a child and leave her screaming.

> 'Labyrinths' – complex; maze-like.
>
> The novella takes a very psychological turn here as it wanders into the world of dreams and nightmares. Knowledge and ignorance; mystery and awareness. Fear is the overriding mood that runs throughout the novella.
>
> Science is facts and figures, reason, truth and reality. The opposite is the supernatural, dreams, the psychological mind as opposed to the physical mind. Emotions and the spirit realm. Dreams and nightmares – duality.
>
> RLS repeats the appalling sight of the little girl being trampled, but frames this in the nightmarish narrative of Utterson's terrifying fearful dreams.

And still the figure had no face by which he might know it; even in his dreams, it had no face, or one that baffled him and melted before his eyes; and thus it was that there sprang up and grew apace in the lawyer's mind a singularly strong, almost an inordinate, curiosity to behold the features of the real

Mr. Hyde. If he could but once set eyes on him, he thought the mystery would lighten and perhaps roll altogether away, as was the habit of mysterious things when well examined. He might see a reason for his friend's strange preference or bondage (call it which you please) and even for the startling clause of the will. At least it would be a face worth seeing: the face of a man who was without bowels of mercy: a face which had but to show itself to raise up, in the mind of the unimpressionable Enfield, a spirit of enduring hatred.

> 'Bondage' – slavery, captivity, suppression, repression. Oppression.
>
> 'Unimpressionable' – not easily influenced, does not give in.
>
> 'Hatred' means to abhor, detest, it stems from FEAR. We hate what we are afraid of. MCM live their lives, buffered by wealth. They are safe in their 'citadels of medicine' – citadel meaning fortress,

From that time forward, Mr. Utterson began to haunt the door in the by-street of shops. In the morning before office hours, at noon when business was plenty and time scarce, at night under the face of the fogged city moon, by all lights and at all hours of solitude or concourse, the lawyer was to be found on his chosen post.

"If he be Mr. Hyde," he had thought, "I shall be Mr. Seek."

And at last his patience was rewarded. It was a fine dry night; frost in the air; the streets as clean as a ballroom floor; the lamps, unshaken by any wind, drawing a regular pattern of light and shadow. By ten o'clock, when the shops were closed, the by-street was very solitary and, in spite of the low growl of London from all round, very silent.

> Pathetic fallacy – clear floor, and fine night anticipate truth and knowledge.
>
> 'light and shadow' – knowledge and ignorance, mystery and secrets, good and evil.
>
> 'low growl' – menace, foreboding, feral, wild, beast, monster.

Small sounds carried far; domestic sounds out of the houses were clearly audible on either side of the roadway; and the rumour of the approach of any passenger preceded him by a long time. Mr. Utterson had been some minutes at his post, when he was aware of an odd light footstep drawing near. In the course of his nightly patrols, he had long grown accustomed to the quaint effect with which the footfalls of a single person, while he is still a great way off, suddenly spring out distinct from the vast hum and clatter of the city. Yet his attention had never before been so sharply and decisively arrested; and it was with a strong, superstitious prevision of success that he withdrew into the entry of the court.

The steps drew swiftly nearer, and swelled out suddenly louder as they turned the end of the street. The lawyer, looking forth from the entry, could soon see what manner of man he had to deal with. He was small and very plainly dressed and the look of him, even at that distance, went somehow strongly against the watcher's inclination. But he made straight for the door, crossing the roadway to save time; and as he came, he drew a key from his pocket like one approaching home.

Mr. Utterson stepped out and touched him on the shoulder as he passed. "Mr. Hyde, I think?"

Mr. Hyde shrank back with a hissing intake of the breath. But his fear was only momentary; and though he did not look the lawyer in the face, he answered coolly enough: "That is my name. What do you want?"

> Setting and sound are used to illustrate Utterson's obsession with Hyde. We are told he paces the streets of London in search of the man. The streets at night are 'as clean as a ballroom floor' – clean and deserted and pristine, the city 'growls' suggesting a warning of imminent danger and 'sounds carried far' highlighting how empty of life the London streets are and giving a sense of danger as Utterson is unwatched and therefore unprotected.
>
> Animalism in the verb 'hissing' – snake, evil, sneaky, sly.

"I see you are going in," returned the lawyer. "I am an old friend of Dr. Jekyll's—Mr. Utterson of Gaunt Street—you must have heard of my name; and meeting you so conveniently, I thought you might admit me."

"You will not find Dr. Jekyll; he is from home," replied Mr. Hyde, blowing in the key. And then suddenly, but still without looking up, "How did you know me?" he asked.

> Utterson's first meeting with Hyde shows them as both being stand-offish, wary and defensive. Hyde is incredibly taken aback by Utterson and Utterson is already predisposed to dislike Hyde as he thinks he is blackmailing Jekyll. Hyde also represents Utterson's fears.

"On your side," said Mr. Utterson "will you do me a favour?"

"With pleasure," replied the other. "What shall it be?"

"Will you let me see your face?" asked the lawyer.

Mr. Hyde appeared to hesitate, and then, as if upon some sudden reflection, fronted about with an air of defiance; and the pair stared at each other pretty fixedly for a few seconds. "Now I shall know you again," said Mr. Utterson. "It may be useful."

"Yes," returned Mr. Hyde, "It is as well we have met; and *à propos*, you should have my address." And he gave a number of a street in Soho.

"Good God!" thought Mr. Utterson, "can he, too, have been thinking of the will?" But he kept his feelings to himself and only grunted in acknowledgment of the address.

"And now," said the other, "how did you know me?"

"By description," was the reply.

"Whose description?"

"We have common friends," said Mr. Utterson.

"Common friends," echoed Mr. Hyde, a little hoarsely. "Who are they?"

"Jekyll, for instance," said the lawyer.

"He never told you," cried Mr. Hyde, with a flush of anger. "I did not think you would have lied."

"Come," said Mr. Utterson, "that is not fitting language."

> Utterson, upon hearing his address – has connected Hyde's need to inform him of his Soho address with the fact that he knows he is entitled through the Will. It is a mutual agreed upon Will therefore as opposed to just Jekyll leaving all his money to the ignorant Hyde.
>
> Note the change in personal pronouns – he to I.
>
> Hyde comes across as unpredictable, misbehaved, erratic, emotional, aggressive, uncivilised.
>
> 'A propos' – on that note

The other snarled aloud into a savage laugh; and the next moment, with extraordinary quickness, he had unlocked the door and disappeared into the house.

> Hyde is described as 'The Other' – because he is the other of all of us – links to theme of duality.
>
> Animalistic verbs of snarled, savage – feral, wild, dangerous, predatory – so the other is all these things – duality of man's nature.

The lawyer stood awhile when Mr. Hyde had left him, the picture of disquietude. Then he began slowly to mount the street, pausing every step or two and putting his hand to his brow like a man in mental perplexity. The problem he was thus debating as he walked, was one of a class that is rarely solved.

> 'Of a class' – this clearly connects Hyde with the phenomena that is the rising of the lower classes. MCM do not fear their own evil, but they fear other things. A challenge from the lower orders is one of their biggest fears at this time.

Mr. Hyde was pale and dwarfish, he gave an impression of deformity without any nameable malformation, he had a displeasing smile, he had borne himself to the lawyer with a sort of murderous mixture of timidity and boldness, and he spoke with a husky, whispering and somewhat broken voice; all these were points against him, but not all of these together could explain the hitherto unknown disgust, loathing and fear with which Mr. Utterson regarded him.

> Hyde is described in a very non descriptive way. He is therefore a concept, a mix of symbolic representation rather than an actual man. His duality comes through here – the primeval aspect of man, the contextual connection with Darwin and his theory. He is also defined greatly by the effect he has on others.

"There must be something else," said the perplexed gentleman. "There *is* something more, if I could find a name for it. God bless me, the man seems hardly human! Something troglodytic, shall we say? or can it be the old story of Dr. Fell? or is it the mere radiance of a foul soul that thus transpires through, and transfigures, its clay continent? The last, I think; for, O my poor old Harry Jekyll, if ever I read Satan's signature upon a face, it is on that of your new friend."

> 'Dr Fell' is an unpleasant person who causes feelings of dislike which are difficult to give any obvious reason for.
>
> 'Troglodytic' – primitive, prehistoric, primeval, precivilisation.
>
> 'Transfigures' – transformed.
>
> 'Clay continent' – the human body.
>
> 'Satan' – religious entity, evil, corrupt and immoral.

Round the corner from the by-street, there was a square of ancient, handsome houses, now for the most part decayed from their high estate and let in flats and chambers to all sorts and conditions of men; map-engravers, architects, shady lawyers and the agents of obscure enterprises.

> This is a clear metaphor for the rise of the lower classes – foreshadowing the end of the corrupt middle/upper classes.
>
> 'ancient, handsome' – Jekyll is describing the higher classes. 'decayed' – connotes immorality, rotting, dying out, corrupted, dead.

One house, however, second from the corner, was still occupied entire; and at the door of this, which wore a great air of wealth and comfort, though it was now plunged in darkness except for the fanlight, Mr. Utterson stopped and knocked. A well-dressed, elderly servant opened the door.

"Is Dr. Jekyll at home, Poole?" asked the lawyer.

"I will see, Mr. Utterson," said Poole, admitting the visitor, as he spoke, into a large, low-roofed, comfortable hall paved with flags, warmed (after the fashion of a country house) by a bright, open fire, and furnished with costly cabinets of oak. "Will you wait here by the fire, sir? or shall I give you a light in the dining-room?"

> This is the public, external face of the MCM. Warm, friendly, wealthy, appearance v reality.

"Here, thank you," said the lawyer, and he drew near and leaned on the tall fender. This hall, in which he was now left alone, was a pet fancy of his friend the doctor's; and Utterson himself was wont to speak of it as the pleasantest room in London. But tonight there was a shudder in his blood; the face of Hyde sat heavy on his memory; he felt (what was rare with him) a nausea and distaste of life; and in the gloom of his spirits, he seemed to read a menace in the flickering of the firelight on the polished cabinets and the uneasy starting of the shadow on the roof. He was ashamed of his relief, when Poole presently returned to announce that Dr. Jekyll was gone out.

> The hallway in the entrance of Jekyll's house was once clean and pleasing to Utterson. After having met and known of Hyde, his perception of the hallway has changed – Duality
>
> He sees aspects of Hyde everywhere.

"I saw Mr. Hyde go in by the old dissecting room, Poole," he said. "Is that right, when Dr. Jekyll is from home?"

"Quite right, Mr. Utterson, sir," replied the servant. "Mr. Hyde has a key."

"Your master seems to repose a great deal of trust in that young man, Poole," resumed the other musingly.

"Yes, sir, he does indeed," said Poole. "We have all orders to obey him."

"I do not think I ever met Mr. Hyde?" asked Utterson.

"O, dear no, sir. He never *dines* here," replied the butler. "Indeed we see very little of him on this side of the house; he mostly comes and goes by the laboratory."

"Well, good-night, Poole."

"Good-night, Mr. Utterson."

And the lawyer set out homeward with a very heavy heart. "Poor Harry Jekyll," he thought, "my mind misgives me he is in deep waters! He was wild when he was young; a long while ago to be sure; but in the law of God, there is no statute of limitations.

> Utterson is not averse to telling lies to Poole. He has just met Hyde, but says that he has not met Hyde.
>
> Poole states that Hyde never dines here, implying that Utterson would only have known him had they dined together. The irony being that Utterson HAS dined with Hyde, in the form of Jekyll.
>
> A statute of limitations is a law that sets a time limit for filing criminal charges against someone. After the time limit has passed, that individual cannot be prosecuted, tried, or punished regardless of the evidence against them. Utterson rightly implies that in Christianity, reckoning and accountability comes to all.

Ay, it must be that; the ghost of some old sin, the cancer of some concealed disgrace: punishment coming, *pede claudo*, years after memory has forgotten and self-love condoned the fault."

The hypocrisy of MCM – having committed a lifetime of terrible sins, they forget in their old age and then argue later that it was all good fun and therefore acceptable.

Oftentimes, old age pulls a mantle of respectability over the misdemeanours of youth. This is exactly what Utterson means here.

'Pede claudo' means punishment comes limping, meaning your sins will catch up with you eventually – Accountability.

And the lawyer, scared by the thought, brooded awhile on his own past, groping in all the corners of memory, least by chance some Jack-in-the-Box of an old iniquity should leap to light there. His past was fairly blameless; few men could read the rolls of their life with less apprehension; yet he was humbled to the dust by the many ill things he had done, and raised up again into a sober and fearful gratitude by the many he had come so near to doing yet avoided.

This paragraph absolutely states that Mr Utterson may be wearing a cover of respectability now because of his age but he has not lived a blameless life. He too has done terrible things, but the way that RLS puts this across is to categorically denounce the hypocrisy if MCM. They do not consider that they have done anything wrong.

'Grope' and' jack in the box' – connote fear, suspense, violence, menace.

And then by a return on his former subject, he conceived a spark of hope. "This Master Hyde, if he were studied," thought he, "must have secrets of his own; black secrets, by the look of him; secrets compared to which poor Jekyll's worst would be like sunshine. Things cannot continue as they are. It turns me cold to think of this creature stealing like a thief to Harry's bedside; poor Harry, what a wakening! And the danger of it; for if this Hyde suspects the existence of the will, he may grow impatient to inherit. Ay, I must put my shoulders to the wheel—if Jekyll will but let me," he added, "if Jekyll will only let me." For once more he saw before his mind's eye, as clear as transparency, the strange clauses of the will.

Utterson is unnerved and unsettled because someone has power over Jekyll. The MCM felt they were above reproach and above accountability. They were in a position of complete power and control and any challenge to that would have been fearful to them.

Utterson thinks that if he can find something incriminating re Hyde, he can use it to control him. The Will however puts Hyde at an advantage. Again, knowledge leads to further mystery.

# 3: Dr. Jekyll Was Quite At Ease

A fortnight later, by excellent good fortune, the doctor gave one of his pleasant dinners to some five or six old cronies, all intelligent, reputable men and all judges of good wine; and Mr. Utterson so contrived that he remained behind after the others had departed.

---

This paragraph contains the main themes of the novella – wealth, solidarity, immorality and the hypocritical MCM.

'Cronies' means allies, friends, followers.

'judges of good wine' mean they all like doing bad things.

---

This was no new arrangement, but a thing that had befallen many scores of times. Where Utterson was liked, he was liked well. Hosts loved to detain the dry lawyer, when the light-hearted and loose-tongued had already their foot on the threshold; they liked to sit a while in his unobtrusive company, practising for solitude, sobering their minds in the man's rich silence after the expense and strain of gaiety.

---

Because Utterson practices silence to the utmost, others sit by him and in this way, they too learn to stay silent. They like him because they feel safe with him, because he protects them.

'Rich' and 'expense' – these are fiscal/financial terms highlighting that it is the wealth of the MCM which enables their oppression and abuse.

Hypocrisy – they may look 'dry' but this is not how they act. Later, Utterson reads a 'dry divinity'.

---

To this rule, Dr. Jekyll was no exception; and as he now sat on the opposite side of the fire—a large, well-made, smooth-faced man of fifty, with something of a slyish cast perhaps, but every mark of capacity and kindness—you could see by his looks that he cherished for Mr. Utterson a sincere and warm affection.

---

'Smooth faced' is repeated with the landlady of the Soho residence of Hyde. There it is associated with hypocrisy – RLS hinting at the hypocrisy of Jekyll.

This is our first introduction of Jekyll.

'Sly' means crafty, furtive, devious, cunning – hints at a darker side to his character.

This is our first meeting of Dr Jekyll. RLS has delayed our meeting so he can properly separate Jekyll and Hyde. The primary plot twist comes out of the shock that they are one, so RLS needs to emphasise their separate existence for the twist to work effectively.

---

"I have been wanting to speak to you, Jekyll," began the latter. "You know that will of yours?"

A close observer might have gathered that the topic was distasteful; but the doctor carried it off gaily. "My poor Utterson," said he, "you are unfortunate in such a client. I never saw a man so distressed as you were by my will; unless it were that hide-bound pedant, Lanyon, at what he called my scientific heresies. O, I know he's a good fellow—you needn't frown—an excellent fellow, and I always mean to see more of him; but a hide-bound pedant for all that; an ignorant, blatant pedant. I was never more disappointed in any man than Lanyon."

> 'hide-bound pedant' – narrow minded and conventional in thinking.
>
> 'hide' – thick impenetrable skin; is a homophone for Hyde.
>
> Jekyll does not like Lanyon that much is clear.

"You know I never approved of it," pursued Utterson, ruthlessly disregarding the fresh topic.

"My will? Yes, certainly, I know that," said the doctor, a trifle sharply. "You have told me so."

"Well, I tell you so again," continued the lawyer. "I have been learning something of young Hyde."

> Reference to Hyde has brought tension between the two men after such a jovial dinner party.

The large handsome face of Dr. Jekyll grew pale to the very lips, and there came a blackness about his eyes. "I do not care to hear more," said he. "This is a matter I thought we had agreed to drop."

> Foreshadowing Hyde in Jekyll – pale, blackness. Clearly, he is distressed at reference to Hyde. Jekyll is a character who is deeply conflicted. His duality, instead of bringing him harmony, has destroyed his peace.
>
> Dr Jekyll is defined as being in conflict. That is the heart of his character.
>
> Theme of Silence.

"What I heard was abominable," said Utterson.

"It can make no change. You do not understand my position," returned the doctor, with a certain incoherency of manner. "I am painfully situated, Utterson; my position is a very strange—a very strange one. It is one of those affairs that cannot be mended by talking."

> Utterson is going against the grain here by asking Jekyll what is going on. Jekyll re-establishes the silence of MCM.

"Jekyll," said Utterson, "you know me: I am a man to be trusted. Make a clean breast of this in confidence; and I make no doubt I can get you out of it."

"My good Utterson," said the doctor, "this is very good of you, this is downright good of you, and I cannot find words to thank you in. I believe you fully; I would trust you before any man alive, ay, before myself, if I could make the choice; but indeed it isn't what you fancy; it is not as bad as that; and just to put your good heart at rest, I will tell you one thing: the moment I choose, I can be rid of Mr. Hyde. I give you my hand upon that; and I thank you again and again; and I will just add one little word, Utterson, that I'm sure you'll take in good part: this is a private matter, and I beg of you to let it sleep."

Utterson reflected a little, looking in the fire.

"I have no doubt you are perfectly right," he said at last, getting to his feet.

"Well, but since we have touched upon this business, and for the last time I hope," continued the doctor, "there is one point I should like you to understand. I have really a very great interest in poor Hyde. I know you have seen him; he told me so; and I fear he was rude. But I do sincerely take a great, a very great interest in that young man; and if I am taken away, Utterson, I wish you to promise me that you will bear with him and get his rights for him. I think you would, if you knew all; and it would be a weight off my mind if you would promise."

"I can't pretend that I shall ever like him," said the lawyer.

"I don't ask that," pleaded Jekyll, laying his hand upon the other's arm; "I only ask for justice; I only ask you to help him for my sake, when I am no longer here."

Utterson heaved an irrepressible sigh. "Well," said he, "I promise."

# 4: The Carew Murder Case

Nearly a year later, in the month of October, 18—, London was startled by a crime of singular ferocity and rendered all the more notable by the high position of the victim. The details were few and startling. A maid servant living alone in a house not far from the river, had gone upstairs to bed about eleven. Although a fog rolled over the city in the small hours, the early part of the night was cloudless, and the lane, which the maid's window overlooked, was brilliantly lit by the full moon.

> Repetition of the verb 'startled' – frightened, surprised, amazed, shocked.
>
> Duality in that there are positive and negative connotations.
>
> Pathetic fallacy – 'fog' connotes concealment, mystery, fear, terror, menace.
>
> 'full moon' – connotes female, and therefore vulnerability, supernatural, mystery, fear, terror.

It seems she was romantically given, for she sat down upon her box, which stood immediately under the window, and fell into a dream of musing. Never (she used to say, with streaming tears, when she narrated that experience), never had she felt more at peace with all men or thought more kindly of the world.

> The setting as laid out by Stevenson is idyllic, calm and filled with love and dreams, the maid is innocent and vulnerable. This is to contrast against the evil of Hyde. To make it more impactful. Follows the conventions of the Gothic genre.

And as she so sat she became aware of an aged beautiful gentleman with white hair, drawing near along the lane; and advancing to meet him, another and very small gentleman, to whom at first she paid less attention. When they had come within speech (which was just under the maid's eyes) the older man bowed and accosted the other with a very pretty manner of politeness. It did not seem as if the subject of his address were of great importance; indeed, from his pointing, it sometimes appeared as if he were only inquiring his way; but the moon shone on his face as he spoke, and the girl was pleased to watch it, it seemed to breathe such an innocent and old-world kindness of disposition, yet with something high too, as of a well-founded self-content. Presently her eye wandered to the other, and she was surprised to recognise in him a certain Mr. Hyde, who had once visited her master and for whom she had conceived a dislike.

> Again, the juxtaposition of the beatific, frail, delicate, good, kind and polite old man against the hideous and violent Hyde is made all the sharper by having them be witnessed by the innocent maid.
>
> The alliteration of 'and so she sat' emphasises peace and harmony to be juxtaposed against the violence that is yet to come.
>
> The maid recognises Hyde as having once visited her master. On a symbolic level, this shows that all MCM across the board consort with Hyde, he is a part of all of them, indeed, all of us.

He had in his hand a heavy cane, with which he was trifling; but he answered never a word, and seemed to listen with an ill-contained impatience. And then all of a sudden he broke out in a great flame of anger, stamping with his foot, brandishing the cane, and carrying on (as the maid described it) like a madman. The old gentleman took a step back, with the air of one very much surprised and a trifle hurt; and at that Mr. Hyde broke out of all bounds and clubbed him to the earth. And next moment, with ape-like fury, he was trampling his victim under foot and hailing down a storm of blows, under which the bones were audibly shattered and the body jumped upon the roadway. At the horror of these sights and sounds, the maid fainted.

> Hyde behaves in a way that is contrary to having manners. Societal expectations at this time maintain that people of the higher classes should have excellent manners. Hyde does not care for manners; he does not care how he acts. He is completely out of control, with no nod to societal expectations.
>
> The brutal murder here hints at the violent acts committed by MCM.
>
> The fear, the terror, the violence; it is all emphasised in this extract. As is the animalistic nature of Hyde. It is very visceral and the sound effects of the breaking of bones makes it all the more sensorially real.
>
> Ape like fury – rage, feral, wild, uncivilised, brute force, uncontrolled. Links to Darwin's theory. Such is the violence that the poor maid is overcome. Contrast.
>
> The unprovoked nature of his attack conveys the meaningless nature of violence, that it is beyond reason.

It was two o'clock when she came to herself and called for the police. The murderer was gone long ago; but there lay his victim in the middle of the lane, incredibly mangled. The stick with which the deed had been done, although it was of some rare and very tough and heavy wood, had broken in the middle under the stress of this insensate cruelty; and one splintered half had rolled in the neighbouring gutter—the other, without doubt, had been carried away by the murderer.

> The broken stick is now a clue, and the two halves connect the crime to the criminal.
>
> The passage of time makes for the murder of Danvers Carew all the more poignant that he has being lying in the street, undiscovered.

A purse and gold watch were found upon the victim: but no cards or papers, except a sealed and stamped envelope, which he had been probably carrying to the post, and which bore the name and address of Mr. Utterson.

> The crime is not motivated by greed. It is therefore an unprovoked crime, for no purpose other than to hurt, maim and kill and destroy out of pure rage. The letter will bring in Utterson and connect them together.

This was brought to the lawyer the next morning, before he was out of bed; and he had no sooner seen it and been told the circumstances, than he shot out a solemn lip. "I shall say nothing till I have seen the body," said he; "this may be very serious. Have the kindness to wait while I dress." And with the same grave countenance he hurried through his breakfast and drove to the police station, whither the body had been carried. As soon as he came into the cell, he nodded.

> Utterson maintaining his silence.

"Yes," said he, "I recognise him. I am sorry to say that this is Sir Danvers Carew."

"Good God, sir," exclaimed the officer, "is it possible?" And the next moment his eye lighted up with professional ambition. "This will make a deal of noise," he said. "And perhaps you can help us to the man." And he briefly narrated what the maid had seen, and showed the broken stick.

> 'his eye lighted up with professional ambition' – police at this time would have been recruited from the lower classes since the middle and upper classes had no need to work. They would therefore, feel no loyalty and would be happy to expose the dark secrets of these MCM.

Mr. Utterson had already quailed at the name of Hyde; but when the stick was laid before him, he could doubt no longer; broken and battered as it was, he recognised it for one that he had himself presented many years before to Henry Jekyll.

> The stick – a symbol of friendship has now become a symbol of murder and violence.
>
> The maid knew it was Hyde. She named him to the police who have named him to Utterson.

"Is this Mr. Hyde a person of small stature?" he inquired.

"Particularly small and particularly wicked-looking, is what the maid calls him," said the officer.

Mr. Utterson reflected; and then, raising his head, "If you will come with me in my cab," he said, "I think I can take you to his house."

It was by this time about nine in the morning, and the first fog of the season.

> 'First fog' – alliteration and pathetic fallacy to denote mystery, secrets, fear, foreboding.

A great chocolate-coloured pall lowered over heaven, but the wind was continually charging and routing these embattled vapours; so that as the cab crawled from street to street, Mr. Utterson beheld a marvellous number of degrees and hues of twilight; for here it would be dark like the back-end of evening; and there would be a glow of a rich, lurid brown, like the light of some strange conflagration; and here, for a moment, the fog would be quite broken up, and a haggard shaft of daylight would glance in between the swirling wreaths.

> Chocolate is not an indigenous word to Victorian England – it has come from the colonies. MCM made their wealth from investment in the colonies, and they also went to these colonies and committed the most appalling immoral acts.
>
> 'pall' – is a cloth that is spread over a coffin, so connotes, death.
>
> The novella uses the weather as metaphors for power and control. Wind is a wild, oppressive force. Embattled vapours denote weakness and its powerlessness. Duality and control.
>
> Use of light and dark reflect knowledge and ignorance and secrecy and mystery. All of which convey an atmosphere of fear and foreboding.

The dismal quarter of Soho seen under these changing glimpses, with its muddy ways, and slatternly passengers, and its lamps, which had never been extinguished or had been kindled afresh to combat this mournful reinvasion of darkness, seemed, in the lawyer's eyes, like a district of some city in a nightmare.

> Soho represents another aspect of London, since London itself is a metaphor for the duality of man. It is poor, dirty and resistant to change. To Utterson, it is a nightmare compared to his fairy tale life of comfort and wealth.

The thoughts of his mind, besides, were of the gloomiest dye; and when he glanced at the companion of his drive, he was conscious of some touch of that terror of the law and the law's officers, which may at times assail the most honest.

> 'touch of that terror of the law and the law's officers, which may at times assail the most honest' – why would any honest individual be afraid of the law? Hypocrisy.
>
> 'Gloomiest dye' – stain, colour, tint.

As the cab drew up before the address indicated, the fog lifted a little and showed him a dingy street, a gin palace, a low French eating house, a shop for the retail of penny numbers and twopenny salads, many ragged children huddled in the doorways, and many women of many different nationalities passing out, key in hand, to have a morning glass; and the next moment the fog settled down again upon that part, as brown as umber, and cut him off from his blackguardly surroundings.

> "many women of many different nationalities" – hints at colonialism. Men were not just abusing low class women but going abroad and abusing and exploiting the women of the colonies.
>
> The use of the phrase "passing out" could be interpreted in multiple ways—it could mean leaving a particular place or losing consciousness
>
> "morning glass" – means duality. Morning is fresh, new, clean. Glass is alcohol.

> This quote could be seen as an exploration of the dualities present in human behaviour—public versus private, conventional versus unconventional. It prompts readers to consider the façades people present to the world versus the hidden aspects of their lives. The juxtaposition of the ordinary act of having a morning drink with the diverse backgrounds of the women, inviting readers to consider themes of identity, societal expectations, and the complexities of human behaviour.
>
> 'blackguardly' – dishonest, dishonourable, deceptive, immoral.

This was the home of Henry Jekyll's favourite; of a man who was heir to a quarter of a million sterling.

> This gives us an indication of the wealth that is at stake here. There is a sharp contrast in that the abject poverty being described to us as being the place where Hyde lives. Hyde could potentially live somewhere in a better area. Stevenson is effectively connecting Hyde as being the evil in man, and the evil in man thrives and indulges itself in these poverty-stricken areas where the women are so desperate for money that they will offer no resistance to whatever abuse is levelled to them. Poverty has made them desperate. The rich abuse them because they can.
>
> Note the class difference in the alcohol – the MCM drink wine, the poor drink gin.

An ivory-faced and silvery-haired old woman opened the door. She had an evil face, smoothed by hypocrisy: but her manners were excellent. Yes, she said, this was Mr. Hyde's, but he was not at home; he had been in that night very late, but he had gone away again in less than an hour; there was nothing strange in that; his habits were very irregular, and he was often absent; for instance, it was nearly two months since she had seen him till yesterday.

> Stevenson uses very clever use of transferred epithets across the text. Here he connects the adjective 'smooth' with the noun 'hypocrisy'. So earlier, when Jekyll was described as smooth faced, we can now attach hypocrisy to him.
>
> This is the same with the 'silvery-haired' – Dr Lanyon and Sir Danvers both also have white hair. This old lady is evil but has excellent manners – she is a metaphor for MCM.

"Very well, then, we wish to see his rooms," said the lawyer; and when the woman began to declare it was impossible, "I had better tell you who this person is," he added. "This is Inspector Newcomen of Scotland Yard."

> Note how Utterson does not give his own name but introduces the inspector by name. Secrecy.

A flash of odious joy appeared upon the woman's face. "Ah!" said she, "he is in trouble! What has he done?"

Mr. Utterson and the inspector exchanged glances. "He don't seem a very popular character," observed the latter. "And now, my good woman, just let me and this gentleman have a look about us."

> The lower classes exposing the evils of the evils of MCM.

In the whole extent of the house, which but for the old woman remained otherwise empty, Mr. Hyde had only used a couple of rooms; but these were furnished with luxury and good taste. A closet was filled with wine; the plate was of silver, the napery elegant; a good picture hung upon the walls, a gift (as Utterson supposed) from Henry Jekyll, who was much of a connoisseur; and the carpets were of many plies and agreeable in colour. At this moment, however, the rooms bore every mark of having been recently and hurriedly ransacked; clothes lay about the floor, with their pockets inside out; lock-fast drawers stood open; and on the hearth there lay a pile of grey ashes, as though many papers had been burned. From these embers the inspector disinterred the butt end of a green cheque book, which had resisted the action of the fire; the other half of the stick was found behind the door; and as this clinched his suspicions, the officer declared himself delighted. A visit to the bank, where several thousand pounds were found to be lying to the murderer's credit, completed his gratification.

> Jekyll's things and his wealth are evident in this seedy hotel-Duality. Also connecting the two.
>
> The discovery of the stick confirms Hyde as being the murderer.
>
> 'plate' – means crockery and dishes.
>
> 'Napery' – tablecloth
>
> It seems that Jekyll transferred his wealth to an account owned by Edward Hyde.

"You may depend upon it, sir," he told Mr. Utterson: "I have him in my hand. He must have lost his head, or he never would have left the stick or, above all, burned the cheque book. Why, money's life to the man. We have nothing to do but wait for him at the bank, and get out the handbills."

This last, however, was not so easy of accomplishment; for Mr. Hyde had numbered few familiars—even the master of the servant maid had only seen him twice; his family could nowhere be traced; he had never been photographed; and the few who could describe him differed widely, as common observers will. Only on one point were they agreed; and that was the haunting sense of unexpressed deformity with which the fugitive impressed his beholders.

> Duality. Money.
>
> The last line confirms that Hyde is not so much a person, as he is a representation of various things to various people. The lack of a definite description also taps the theme of unknown and mystery, creating more fear and menace.

# 5: Incident of the Letter

It was late in the afternoon, when Mr. Utterson found his way to Dr. Jekyll's door, where he was at once admitted by Poole, and carried down by the kitchen offices and across a yard which had once been a garden, to the building which was indifferently known as the laboratory or dissecting rooms. The doctor had bought the house from the heirs of a celebrated surgeon; and his own tastes being rather chemical than anatomical, had changed the destination of the block at the bottom of the garden. It was the first time that the lawyer had been received in that part of his friend's quarters; and he eyed the dingy, windowless structure with curiosity, and gazed round with a distasteful sense of strangeness as he crossed the theatre, once crowded with eager students and now lying gaunt and silent, the tables laden with chemical apparatus, the floor strewn with crates and littered with packing straw, and the light falling dimly through the foggy cupola.

---

The anatomical theatre belonged to 'Denman' who, being a man of the primeval den, denotes investigating the primitive nature of humankind.

Jekyll's departure from 'anatomical' to the 'chemical'; his movement from the dissecting table to the chemistry set, is symbolic of his differences to Lanyon. Jekyll, we later discover, is exploring human nature through 'transcendental medicine', which is a 'modern' form of alchemy; This can also be seen as Dr Jekyll having discarded traditional science in pursuit of the mystical. Alchemy is a medieval forerunner of chemistry. At its heart was the pursuit of changing one element into another. Alchemists were famous for seeking to turn base metal into gold. This further connotes the supernatural and surrealism.

The noun 'strangeness' is echoed in the novella's title and brings tension; the 'dingy, windowless structure' symbolises the dark depths to which Jekyll sinks and intensifies the sense of malevolence. The contrast between the energetic 'crowded with eager students' and the 'gaunt and silent' theatre presents a fearful impression of death; the symbolic dimness and fog denotes a lost soul.

'dingy, windowless structure with curiosity'

'light falling dimly through the foggy cupola'

Cupola is a roof or part of a roof that is shaped like a dome, made of glass. 'Foggy' means concealed, cloudy.

Knowledge is shrouded with mystery.

---

At the further end, a flight of stairs mounted to a door covered with red baize; and through this, Mr. Utterson was at last received into the doctor's cabinet.

---

'red baize door' – red denotes danger. Baize is a thick felt, the kind used on snooker tables. Baize was typically to be found on doors that separated the family's living quarters with those of the servants, so therefore represents class separation.

---

It was a large room fitted round with glass presses, furnished, among other things, with a cheval-glass and a business table, and looking out upon the court by three dusty windows barred with iron. The fire burned in the grate; a lamp was set lighted on the chimney shelf, for even in the houses the fog began to lie thickly; and there, close up to the warmth, sat Dr. Jekyll, looking deathly sick.

> Bars on the window – this has become his physical prison, the room is symbolic of his internal struggle. The good over the evil.

He did not rise to meet his visitor, but held out a cold hand and bade him welcome in a changed voice.

> Later, in chapter 8, Utterson comments on the strangeness of the cheval glass being in the 'cabinet' (private chamber).
>
> The fog is now lying thickly even 'in the houses' and this symbolism, particularly when combined with Jekyll's ill health and the pre-modifying adverb 'deadly', creates a feeling of doom and impending death. Jekyll's 'cold hand' reminds us of other characters' reactions to Hyde. Jekyll's changed voice, whilst shocking here, causes further distress for Utterson and Poole later in the novella. These elements all show that Jekyll is in a very bad way.
>
> 'Cheval-glass' is a full-length mirror that swivels on a frame. This will become very significant towards the end of the novella.
>
> 'in the houses the fog began to lie thickly;' – the inhabitants, duality, houses being metaphors for human bodies, fog denotes evil, malevolence, mystery, corruption, fear.

"And now," said Mr. Utterson, as soon as Poole had left them, "you have heard the news?"

The doctor shuddered. "They were crying it in the square," he said. "I heard them in my dining-room."

"One word," said the lawyer. "Carew was my client, but so are you, and I want to know what I am doing. You have not been mad enough to hide this fellow?"

"Utterson, I swear to God," cried the doctor, "I swear to God I will never set eyes on him again. I bind my honour to you that I am done with him in this world. It is all at an end. And indeed he does not want my help; you do not know him as I do; he is safe, he is quite safe; mark my words, he will never more be heard of."

> Utterson waits till Poole has left the room before he speaks – secrecy especially from the lower classes. They must not know.
>
> 'Safe' – protected, sheltered, opposite of dangerous.
>
> 'Bind' – the tie something to you, to attach one thing to another.

The lawyer listened gloomily; he did not like his friend's feverish manner. "You seem pretty sure of him," said he; "and for your sake, I hope you may be right. If it came to a trial, your name might appear."

> To Utterson, the murder is secondary to the good name of Jekyll. It just shows the value MCM placed on their reputations. They felt they were above the law.
>
> 'Feverish' – sick, unwell, morally more than physically.

"I am quite sure of him," replied Jekyll; "I have grounds for certainty that I cannot share with any one. But there is one thing on which you may advise me. I have—I have received a letter; and I am at a loss whether I should show it to the police. I should like to leave it in your hands, Utterson; you would judge wisely, I am sure; I have so great a trust in you."

"You fear, I suppose, that it might lead to his detection?" asked the lawyer.

"No," said the other. "I cannot say that I care what becomes of Hyde; I am quite done with him. I was thinking of my own character, which this hateful business has rather exposed."

> 'I was thinking of my own character, which this hateful business has rather exposed' – Jekyll speaks almost in a riddle here. Links to Duality.
>
> Despite his frantic and despairing state, Jekyll is still able to muster enough calm to concoct the plan of throwing Utterson off the scent. It shows a duplicitous nature, good and evil.
>
> Jekyll talks about how his own character is exposed. Hyde has been exposed. Hyde is now in the public domain. Jekyll is not. Jekyll is still anonymous, except of course to Utterson.

Utterson ruminated awhile; he was surprised at his friend's selfishness, and yet relieved by it. "Well," said he, at last, "let me see the letter."

> Despite Jekyll's terrified demeanour, he is still able to write the letter and be clear enough in his mind to hand it over. Jekyll is duplicitous, good, and bad/ trust with lies.

The letter was written in an odd, upright hand and signed "Edward Hyde": and it signified, briefly enough, that the writer's benefactor, Dr. Jekyll, whom he had long so unworthily repaid for a thousand generosities, need labour under no alarm for his safety, as he had means of escape on which he placed a sure dependence. The lawyer liked this letter well enough; it put a better colour on the intimacy than he had looked for; and he blamed himself for some of his past suspicions.

"Have you the envelope?" he asked.

"I burned it," replied Jekyll, "before I thought what I was about. But it bore no postmark. The note was handed in."

"Shall I keep this and sleep upon it?" asked Utterson.

"I wish you to judge for me entirely," was the reply. "I have lost confidence in myself."

"Well, I shall consider," returned the lawyer. "And now one word more: it was Hyde who dictated the terms in your will about that disappearance?"

The doctor seemed seized with a qualm of faintness; he shut his mouth tight and nodded.

"I knew it," said Utterson. "He meant to murder you. You had a fine escape."

"I have had what is far more to the purpose," returned the doctor solemnly: "I have had a lesson—O God, Utterson, what a lesson I have had!" And he covered his face for a moment with his hands.

> Jekyll is in a state of conflict. It is, however, self-made.
>
> Jekyll's appeal to God, brings some seriousness and religiosity to his plight. His calling out to God to save him and hiding his face, while he has just lied to Utterson is more about saving his skin than being repentant.

On his way out, the lawyer stopped and had a word or two with Poole. "By the bye," said he, "there was a letter handed in to-day: what was the messenger like?" But Poole was positive nothing had come except by post; "and only circulars by that," he added.

> The irony is that Jekyll's attempts to hide Hyde ultimately leads to his exposure. Had he not said that the letter was handed in, Utterson would not have asked Poole, to be told that no one handed anything in – painting Jekyll as having lied.
>
> Poole the servant exposing Jekyll's secrets.

This news sent off the visitor with his fears renewed. Plainly the letter had come by the laboratory door; possibly, indeed, it had been written in the cabinet; and if that were so, it must be differently judged, and handled with the more caution.

> Utterson's suspicions all continue to lead us to believing that Jekyll and Hyde are two separate individuals and not one. Ironically, he is part of the mystery.

The newsboys, as he went, were crying themselves hoarse along the footways: "Special edition. Shocking murder of an M.P." That was the funeral oration of one friend and client; and he could not help a certain apprehension lest the good name of another should be sucked down in the eddy of the scandal. It was, at least, a ticklish decision that he had to make; and self-reliant as he was by habit, he began to cherish a longing for advice. It was not to be had directly; but perhaps, he thought, it might be fished for.

> 'That was the funeral oration of one friend and client; and he could not help a certain apprehension lest the good name of another should be sucked down in the eddy of the scandal'.
>
> 'A good name' means reputation. A 'scandal' means someone has done something wrong and it has been made public and that society has deemed it unacceptable.

Presently after, he sat on one side of his own hearth, with Mr. Guest, his head clerk, upon the other, and midway between, at a nicely calculated distance from the fire, a bottle of a particular old wine that had long dwelt unsunned in the foundations of his house.

> Utterson is a keeper of fine wine, marking him as a MCM with a taste for the finer things in life: the wine is old and it has been selected because it is a 'particular' one; it is perfectly placed to warm before being drunk; for years, it has been stored in the wine cellar which is 'in the foundations' of the house of wealth; the wine represents maturity, sophistication, culture and elegance. Drinking wine here is associated with being civilised. It also represents immorality since it makes the drinker drunk. It also connects to reference to class in chapter 2 – 'ancient, handsome houses, now for the most part decayed from their high estate'. This class distinction needs to go.

The fog still slept on the wing above the drowned city, where the lamps glimmered like carbuncles; and through the muffle and smother of these fallen clouds, the procession of the town's life was still rolling in through the great arteries with a sound as of a mighty wind. But the room was gay with firelight. In the bottle the acids were long ago resolved; the imperial dye had softened with time, as the colour grows richer in stained windows; and the glow of hot autumn afternoons on hillside vineyards, was ready to be set free and to disperse the fogs of London.

> 'fog' denotes mystery, supernatural, ignorance, duality, sin. It is sleeping, meaning unaware, comatose, latent, unaware. 'The wing' connotes angels, redemption, salvation, purity, love.
>
> The 'drowned city' connotes the fallen world, the gothic, the fin de siècle.
>
> The simile 'like carbuncles' means like precious gemstones; describing the beauty of gaslit streetlamps which shine with the red 'glimmer' of rubies or garnets. This beauty, born of the Industrial Revolution, delicately shines through, despite the never-ending fog of disharmony and corruption that swirls in the sky above.
>
> The fog's clouds have, post-Eden, 'fallen' onto the city with an onomatopoeic 'muffle' and a suffocating 'smother' but they do not extinguish the town's vitality which runs through its artery-like streets 'with a sound as of a mighty wind'.
>
> 'the imperial dye had softened with time, as the colour grows richer in stained windows'
>
> 'reddish hue, began, in proportion as the crystals melted, to brighten in colour, to effervesce audibly, and to throw off small fumes of vapour. Suddenly and at the same moment, the ebullition ceased and the compound changed to a dark purple, which faded again more slowly to a watery green.'

Insensibly the lawyer melted. There was no man from whom he kept fewer secrets than Mr. Guest; and he was not always sure that he kept as many as he meant.

Guest had often been on business to the doctor's; he knew Poole; he could scarce have failed to hear of Mr. Hyde's familiarity about the house; he might draw conclusions: was it not as well, then, that he should see a letter which put that mystery to right? and above all since Guest, being a great student and critic of handwriting, would consider the step natural and obliging? The clerk, besides, was a man of counsel; he could scarce read so strange a document without dropping a remark; and by that remark Mr. Utterson might shape his future course.

"This is a sad business about Sir Danvers," he said.

"Yes, sir, indeed. It has elicited a great deal of public feeling," returned Guest. "The man, of course, was mad."

"I should like to hear your views on that," replied Utterson. "I have a document here in his handwriting; it is between ourselves, for I scarce know what to do about it; it is an ugly business at the best. But there it is; quite in your way: a murderer's autograph."

Guest's eyes brightened, and he sat down at once and studied it with passion. "No sir," he said: "not mad; but it is an odd hand."

"And by all accounts a very odd writer," added the lawyer.

Just then the servant entered with a note.

"Is that from Dr. Jekyll, sir?" inquired the clerk. "I thought I knew the writing. Anything private, Mr. Utterson?"

"Only an invitation to dinner. Why? Do you want to see it?"

"One moment. I thank you, sir;" and the clerk laid the two sheets of paper alongside and sedulously compared their contents. "Thank you, sir," he said at last, returning both; "it's a very interesting autograph."

There was a pause, during which Mr. Utterson struggled with himself. "Why did you compare them, Guest?" he inquired suddenly.

"Well, sir," returned the clerk, "there's a rather singular resemblance; the two hands are in many points identical: only differently sloped."

"Rather quaint," said Utterson.

"It is, as you say, rather quaint," returned Guest.

"I wouldn't speak of this note, you know," said the master.

"No, sir," said the clerk. "I understand."

But no sooner was Mr. Utterson alone that night, than he locked the note into his safe, where it reposed from that time forward. "What!" he thought. "Henry Jekyll forge for a murderer!" And his blood ran cold in his veins.

> Again, ambiguity with the handwriting. Utterson believes that Jekyll has forged Hyde's handwriting. The signature itself represents duality.
>
> Utterson 'struggles' because he's uncomfortable confiding in Guest. He is also afraid of the answer.
>
> Lock – symbolic of secrets and hiding the truth.

## 6: Incident of Dr. Lanyon

Time ran on; thousands of pounds were offered in reward, for the death of Sir Danvers was resented as a public injury; but Mr. Hyde had disappeared out of the ken of the police as though he had never existed. Much of his past was unearthed, indeed, and all disreputable: tales came out of the man's cruelty, at once so callous and violent; of his vile life, of his strange associates, of the hatred that seemed to have surrounded his career; but of his present whereabouts, not a whisper.

> Thousands of pounds were offered for Danvers but for the little girl at the beginning. We screwed him up to a hundred pounds – note the difference in figures. Borne out in the value that is placed on the little girl as opposed to an eminent MCM.

From the time he had left the house in Soho on the morning of the murder, he was simply blotted out; and gradually, as time drew on, Mr. Utterson began to recover from the hotness of his alarm, and to grow more at quiet with himself. The death of Sir Danvers was, to his way of thinking, more than paid for by the disappearance of Mr. Hyde. Now that that evil influence had been withdrawn, a new life began for Dr. Jekyll. He came out of his seclusion, renewed relations with his friends, became once more their familiar guest and entertainer; and whilst he had always been known for charities, he was now no less distinguished for religion. He was busy, he was much in the open air, he did good; his face seemed to open and brighten, as if with an inward consciousness of service; and for more than two months, the doctor was at peace.

> Jekyll doing 'good' has affected this face – it is open and bright, because he is seen to be doing good. He has also become more religious possibly hinting at his guilt-is he more religious because he has a lot of atoning to do?

On the 8th of January Utterson had dined at the doctor's with a small party; Lanyon had been there; and the face of the host had looked from one to the other as in the old days when the trio were inseparable friends. On the 12th, and again on the 14th, the door was shut against the lawyer. "The doctor was confined to the house," Poole said, "and saw no one." On the 15th, he tried again, and was again refused; and having now been used for the last two months to see his friend almost daily, he found this return of solitude to weigh upon his spirits. The fifth night he had in Guest to dine with him; and the sixth he betook himself to Dr. Lanyon's.

There at least he was not denied admittance; but when he came in, he was shocked at the change which had taken place in the doctor's appearance. He had his death-warrant written legibly upon his face. The rosy man had grown pale; his flesh had fallen away; he was visibly balder and older; and yet it was not so much these tokens of a swift physical decay that arrested the lawyer's notice, as a look in the eye and quality of manner that seemed to testify to some deep-seated terror of the mind. It was unlikely that the doctor should fear death; and yet that was what Utterson was tempted to suspect. "Yes," he thought; "he is a doctor, he must know his own state and that his days are counted; and the knowledge is more than he can bear." And yet when Utterson remarked on his ill looks, it was with an air of great firmness that Lanyon declared himself a doomed man.

> Utterson goes to see Lanyon on January 21st.
>
> Dr Lanyon has undergone a huge change.

"I have had a shock," he said, "and I shall never recover. It is a question of weeks. Well, life has been pleasant; I liked it; yes, sir, I used to like it. I sometimes think if we knew all, we should be more glad to get away."

"Jekyll is ill, too," observed Utterson. "Have you seen him?"

But Lanyon's face changed, and he held up a trembling hand. "I wish to see or hear no more of Dr. Jekyll," he said in a loud, unsteady voice. "I am quite done with that person; and I beg that you will spare me any allusion to one whom I regard as dead."

"Tut, tut!" said Mr. Utterson; and then after a considerable pause, "Can't I do anything?" he inquired. "We are three very old friends, Lanyon; we shall not live to make others."

"Nothing can be done," returned Lanyon; "ask himself."

"He will not see me," said the lawyer.

"I am not surprised at that," was the reply. "Some day, Utterson, after I am dead, you may perhaps come to learn the right and wrong of this. I cannot tell you. And in the meantime, if you can sit and talk with me of other things, for God's sake, stay and do so; but if you cannot keep clear of this accursed topic, then in God's name, go, for I cannot bear it."

> Lanyon prophesizes his own death. He says that he has had a shock. Shock means fear. The reader is intrigued by the fact that Jekyll is connected to Lanyon's deteriorated state but is none the wiser. Jekyll must have done something terrible to have this effect.

As soon as he got home, Utterson sat down and wrote to Jekyll, complaining of his exclusion from the house, and asking the cause of this unhappy break with Lanyon; and the next day brought him a long answer, often very pathetically worded, and sometimes darkly mysterious in drift.

> 'Pathetic' means a thing to be pitied; it also means something of a very low standard – duality.
>
> 'Darkly' means threatening, mysterious, ominous – brings a mood of fear.

The quarrel with Lanyon was incurable. "I do not blame our old friend," Jekyll wrote, "but I share his view that we must never meet. I mean from henceforth to lead a life of extreme seclusion; you must not be surprised, nor must you doubt my friendship, if my door is often shut even to you. You must suffer me to go my own dark way. I have brought on myself a punishment and a danger that I cannot name. If I am the chief of sinners, I am the chief of sufferers also. I could not think that this earth contained a place for sufferings and terrors so unmanning; and you can do but one thing, Utterson, to lighten this destiny, and that is to respect my silence." Utterson was amazed; the dark influence of Hyde had been withdrawn, the doctor had returned to his old tasks and amities; a week ago, the prospect had smiled with every promise of a cheerful and an honoured age; and now in a moment, friendship, and peace of mind, and the whole tenor of his life were wrecked. So great and unprepared a change pointed to madness; but in view of Lanyon's manner and words, there must lie for it some deeper ground.

> Alliteration of 'dark' and 'danger' implies a sense of doom and destiny much like Lanyon prophesizing his own death. This suggests the presence of a higher power over which the individual has no control. Evil can take control. If we let it.
>
> Following the theme of silence, Jekyll asks to be allowed to be silent. He accepts all the blame for having placed himself in this position. He is a tormented and conflicted man. He is in a very dangerous position.
>
> The characters because of their silent and secretive nature maintain the mystery.
>
> 'Chief of sinners/chief of sufferers' – this reveals duality, that he is two individuals. The sinner in him is Hyde, the sufferer is Jekyll.

A week afterwards Dr. Lanyon took to his bed, and in something less than a fortnight he was dead. The night after the funeral, at which he had been sadly affected, Utterson locked the door of his business room, and sitting there by the light of a melancholy candle, drew out and set before him an envelope addressed by the hand and sealed with the seal of his dead friend. "PRIVATE: for the hands of G. J. Utterson ALONE, and in case of his predecease *to be destroyed unread*," so it was emphatically superscribed; and the lawyer dreaded to behold the contents. "I have buried one friend to-day," he thought: "what if this should cost me another?" And then he condemned the fear as a disloyalty, and broke the seal. Within there was another enclosure, likewise sealed, and marked upon the cover as "not to be opened till the death or disappearance of Dr. Henry Jekyll." Utterson could not trust his eyes. Yes, it was disappearance; here again, as in the mad will which he had long ago restored to its author, here again were the idea of a disappearance and the name of Henry Jekyll bracketted. But in the will, that idea had sprung from the sinister suggestion of the man Hyde; it was set there with a purpose all too plain and horrible. Written by the hand of Lanyon, what should it mean? A great curiosity came on the trustee, to disregard the prohibition and dive at once to the bottom of these mysteries; but professional honour and faith to his dead friend were stringent obligations; and the packet slept in the inmost corner of his private safe.

> Utterson can be seen to be an essential plotting device as to the sealed letters and the conditions upon which the seals should be broken if at all.
>
> Both Jekyll's Will and Lanyon's letter, are linked with the same terms, connected to the death or disappearance of Jekyll.

It is one thing to mortify curiosity, another to conquer it; and it may be doubted if, from that day forth, Utterson desired the society of his surviving friend with the same eagerness. He thought of him kindly; but his thoughts were disquieted and fearful. He went to call indeed; but he was perhaps relieved to be denied admittance; perhaps, in his heart, he preferred to speak with Poole upon the doorstep and surrounded by the air and sounds of the open city, rather than to be admitted into that house of voluntary bondage, and to sit and speak with its inscrutable recluse. Poole had, indeed, no very pleasant news to communicate.

> Inside and outside, duality.
>
> 'Voluntary bondage' – bondage means the condition of being a slave. Bondage implies a relationship based upon power and control.
>
> 'Voluntary' – that he has done it to himself, no one is to blame but him.
>
> 'Inscrutable' means difficult to read, obscure, it therefore connects to mystery and hidden things.
>
> 'Mortify' – to subdue and repress.

The doctor, it appeared, now more than ever confined himself to the cabinet over the laboratory, where he would sometimes even sleep; he was out of spirits, he had grown very silent, he did not read; it seemed as if he had something on his mind. Utterson became so used to the unvarying character of these reports, that he fell off little by little in the frequency of his visits.

# 7: Incident at the Window

It chanced on Sunday, when Mr. Utterson was on his usual walk with Mr. Enfield, that their way lay once again through the by-street; and that when they came in front of the door, both stopped to gaze on it.

> Cyclical nature of the novella. Another Sunday, and the same by-street.

"Well," said Enfield, "that story's at an end at least. We shall never see more of Mr. Hyde."

"I hope not," said Utterson. "Did I ever tell you that I once saw him, and shared your feeling of repulsion?"

"It was impossible to do the one without the other," returned Enfield. "And by the way, what an ass you must have thought me, not to know that this was a back way to Dr. Jekyll's! It was partly your own fault that I found it out, even when I did."

> This at least satisfies the mystery as to why Enfield did not reveal that it was Jekyll's house in the first chapter. It is mentioned but not clarified, inline with the secretive nature of these MCM.

"So you found it out, did you?" said Utterson. "But if that be so, we may step into the court and take a look at the windows. To tell you the truth, I am uneasy about poor Jekyll; and even outside, I feel as if the presence of a friend might do him good."

The court was very cool and a little damp, and full of premature twilight, although the sky, high up overhead, was still bright with sunset. The middle one of the three windows was half-way open; and sitting close beside it, taking the air with an infinite sadness of mien, like some disconsolate prisoner, Utterson saw Dr. Jekyll.

> The contrast between the cool, damp court and the bright sky convey duality. Sorrow with despair, light with dark, warmth with heat. Pathetic fallacy in 'premature twilight', as well as duality, all convey that Jekyll too is close to death.
>
> 'Mien' – manner and appearance.
>
> Note the positioning of the middle window, halfway – referencing duality. Window also connotes freedom, and choice, and escape.
>
> Dr Jekyll sitting close to the half-opened window shows that he is at the crossroads of good and evil, freedom and imprisonment, choice and compulsion.
>
> The repetition of 'premature' to also describe Lanyon's hair and now the twilight, foreshadows Jekyll's death and the tragic element of the novella. There is a feeling that this will not end well for Jekyll.

"What! Jekyll!" he cried. "I trust you are better."

"I am very low, Utterson," replied the doctor drearily, "very low. It will not last long, thank God."

"You stay too much indoors," said the lawyer. "You should be out, whipping up the circulation like Mr. Enfield and me. (This is my cousin—Mr. Enfield—Dr. Jekyll.) Come now; get your hat and take a quick turn with us."

"You are very good," sighed the other. "I should like to very much; but no, no, no, it is quite impossible; I dare not. But indeed, Utterson, I am very glad to see you; this is really a great pleasure; I would ask you and Mr. Enfield up, but the place is really not fit."

'dare not' – means that he is terrified of the consequences should he come out.

'it will not last' – foreshadowing of a final and bad end.

"Why, then," said the lawyer, good-naturedly, "the best thing we can do is to stay down here and speak with you from where we are."

"That is just what I was about to venture to propose," returned the doctor with a smile. But the words were hardly uttered, before the smile was struck out of his face and succeeded by an expression of such abject terror and despair, as froze the very blood of the two gentlemen below.

'Struck' connotes violence, shock, surprise.

Fear and terror.

They saw it but for a glimpse for the window was instantly thrust down; but that glimpse had been sufficient, and they turned and left the court without a word. In silence, too, they traversed the by-street; and it was not until they had come into a neighbouring thoroughfare, where even upon a Sunday there were still some stirrings of life, that Mr. Utterson at last turned and looked at his companion. They were both pale; and there was an answering horror in their eyes.

"God forgive us, God forgive us," said Mr. Utterson.

But Mr. Enfield only nodded his head very seriously, and walked on once more in silence.

## 8: The Last Night

Mr. Utterson was sitting by his fireside one evening after dinner, when he was surprised to receive a visit from Poole.

"Bless me, Poole, what brings you here?" he cried; and then taking a second look at him, "What ails you?" he added; "is the doctor ill?"

"Mr. Utterson," said the man, "there is something wrong."

"Take a seat, and here is a glass of wine for you," said the lawyer. "Now, take your time, and tell me plainly what you want."

"You know the doctor's ways, sir," replied Poole, "and how he shuts himself up. Well, he's shut up again in the cabinet; and I don't like it, sir—I wish I may die if I like it. Mr. Utterson, sir, I'm afraid."

"Now, my good man," said the lawyer, "be explicit. What are you afraid of?"

"I've been afraid for about a week," returned Poole, doggedly disregarding the question, "and I can bear it no more."

The man's appearance amply bore out his words; his manner was altered for the worse; and except for the moment when he had first announced his terror, he had not once looked the lawyer in the face. Even now, he sat with the glass of wine untasted on his knee, and his eyes directed to a corner of the floor. "I can bear it no more," he repeated.

"Come," said the lawyer, "I see you have some good reason, Poole; I see there is something seriously amiss. Try to tell me what it is."

"I think there's been foul play," said Poole, hoarsely.

"Foul play!" cried the lawyer, a good deal frightened and rather inclined to be irritated in consequence. "What foul play! What does the man mean?"

"I daren't say, sir," was the answer; "but will you come along with me and see for yourself?"

Mr. Utterson's only answer was to rise and get his hat and greatcoat; but he observed with wonder the greatness of the relief that appeared upon the butler's face, and perhaps with no less, that the wine was still untasted when he set it down to follow.

> There is a clear connection to alcohol in the novella. Note how Poole is capable of control and is able to suppress or repress his wild side through not taking the wine. Also, wine is a drink only enjoyed by the higher classes. The fact that the wine has been mentioned three times, makes it significant. Notice also how Utterson is relieved that Poole has not touched the wine. Uttterson does not want the class status quo to be disrupted in any way. Poole must know and stick to his place.
>
> 'Greatcoat' – connotes reputation, external, cover.

It was a wild, cold, seasonable night of March, with a pale moon, lying on her back as though the wind had tilted her, and flying wrack of the most diaphanous and lawny texture. The wind made talking difficult, and flecked the blood into the face.

> Pathetic fallacy in 'wild' and 'cold' – denoting, unwelcoming, harsh, feral, uncomfortable.
>
> 'Seasonable' means usual for the time of year; coming at the right time or perfect for the occasion; opportune.
>
> Both symbolise duality.
>
> 'A pale Moon' – personification; moon is a feminine entity, feminine contextually means to be frail, delicate, weak and vulnerable, made even more so by use of the adjective 'pale' – sickly, weak, frail, close to death. She is even more vulnerable because she is lying on her back, in a submissive and defenceless position.
>
> 'wind' – connotes a wild oppressive force. It is a masculine energy.
>
> 'tilt' – means to lean, to yield, with no resistance.
>
> 'wrack' – means a wrecked ship.
>
> 'diaphanous and lawny' – diaphanous means transparent and see through. lawny is the soft, thin cotton like material lawn, so it's a juxtaposition of clear and milky, knowledge and ignorance.

It seemed to have swept the streets unusually bare of passengers, besides; for Mr. Utterson thought he had never seen that part of London so deserted. He could have wished it otherwise; never in his life had he been conscious of so sharp a wish to see and touch his fellow-creatures; for struggle as he might, there was borne in upon his mind a crushing anticipation of calamity. The square, when they got there, was full of wind and dust, and the thin trees in the garden were lashing themselves along the railing. Poole, who had kept all the way a pace or two ahead, now pulled up in the middle of the pavement, and in spite of the biting weather, took off his hat and mopped his brow with a red pocket-handkerchief. But for all the hurry of his coming, these were not the dews of exertion that he wiped away, but the moisture of some strangling anguish; for his face was white and his voice, when he spoke, harsh and broken.

"Well, sir," he said, "here we are, and God grant there be nothing wrong."

"Amen, Poole," said the lawyer.

Thereupon the servant knocked in a very guarded manner; the door was opened on the chain; and a voice asked from within, "Is that you, Poole?"

"It's all right," said Poole. "Open the door."

The hall, when they entered it, was brightly lighted up; the fire was built high; and about the hearth the whole of the servants, men and women, stood huddled together like a flock of sheep. At the sight of Mr. Utterson, the housemaid broke into hysterical whimpering; and the cook, crying out "Bless God! it's Mr. Utterson," ran forward as if to take him in her arms.

> Utterson is annoyed at the unconventional behaviour of the servants.
>
> The servants are terrified hence the chain on the door. Gothic conventions. Invocation of God. Fear, terror, religion, terrified women,

"What, what? Are you all here?" said the lawyer peevishly. "Very irregular, very unseemly; your master would be far from pleased."

"They're all afraid," said Poole.

Blank silence followed, no one protesting; only the maid lifted her voice and now wept loudly.

"Hold your tongue!" Poole said to her, with a ferocity of accent that testified to his own jangled nerves; and indeed, when the girl had so suddenly raised the note of her lamentation, they had all started and turned towards the inner door with faces of dreadful expectation. "And now," continued the butler, addressing the knife-boy, "reach me a candle, and we'll get this through hands at once." And then he begged Mr. Utterson to follow him, and led the way to the back garden.

"Now, sir," said he, "you come as gently as you can. I want you to hear, and I don't want you to be heard. And see here, sir, if by any chance he was to ask you in, don't go."

Mr. Utterson's nerves, at this unlooked-for termination, gave a jerk that nearly threw him from his balance; but he recollected his courage and followed the butler into the laboratory building through the surgical theatre, with its lumber of crates and bottles, to the foot of the stair. Here Poole motioned him to stand on one side and listen; while he himself, setting down the candle and making a great and obvious call on his resolution, mounted the steps and knocked with a somewhat uncertain hand on the red baize of the cabinet door.

"Mr. Utterson, sir, asking to see you," he called; and even as he did so, once more violently signed to the lawyer to give ear.

A voice answered from within: "Tell him I cannot see anyone," it said complainingly.

"Thank you, sir," said Poole, with a note of something like triumph in his voice; and taking up his candle, he led Mr. Utterson back across the yard and into the great kitchen, where the fire was out and the beetles were leaping on the floor.

"Sir," he said, looking Mr. Utterson in the eyes, "Was that my master's voice?"

"It seems much changed," replied the lawyer, very pale, but giving look for look.

"Changed? Well, yes, I think so," said the butler. "Have I been twenty years in this man's house, to be deceived about his voice? No, sir; master's made away with; he was made away with eight days ago, when we heard him cry out upon the name of God; and *who's* in there instead of him, and *why* it stays there, is a thing that cries to Heaven, Mr. Utterson!"

"This is a very strange tale, Poole; this is rather a wild tale my man," said Mr. Utterson, biting his finger. "Suppose it were as you suppose, supposing Dr. Jekyll to have been—well, murdered, what could induce the murderer to stay? That won't hold water; it doesn't commend itself to reason."

"Well, Mr. Utterson, you are a hard man to satisfy, but I'll do it yet," said Poole. "All this last week (you must know) him, or it, whatever it is that lives in that cabinet, has been crying night and day for some sort of medicine and cannot get it to his mind. It was sometimes his way—the master's, that is—to write his orders on a sheet of paper and throw it on the stair. We've had nothing else this week back; nothing but papers, and a closed door, and the very meals left there to be smuggled in when nobody was looking. Well, sir, every day, ay, and twice and thrice in the same day, there have been orders and complaints, and I have been sent flying to all the wholesale chemists in town. Every time I brought the stuff back, there would be another paper telling me to return it, because it was not pure, and another order to a different firm. This drug is wanted bitter bad, sir, whatever for."

"Have you any of these papers?" asked Mr. Utterson.

Poole felt in his pocket and handed out a crumpled note, which the lawyer, bending nearer to the candle, carefully examined. Its contents ran thus: "Dr. Jekyll presents his compliments to Messrs. Maw. He assures them that their last sample is impure and quite useless for his present purpose. In the year 18—, Dr. J. purchased a somewhat large quantity from Messrs. M. He now begs them to search with most sedulous care, and should any of the same quality be left, forward it to him at once. Expense is no consideration. The importance of this to Dr. J. can hardly be exaggerated." So far the letter had run composedly enough, but here with a sudden splutter of the pen, the writer's emotion had broken loose. "For God's sake," he added, "find me some of the old."

"This is a strange note," said Mr. Utterson; and then sharply, "How do you come to have it open?"

"The man at Maw's was main angry, sir, and he threw it back to me like so much dirt," returned Poole.

"This is unquestionably the doctor's hand, do you know?" resumed the lawyer.

"I thought it looked like it," said the servant rather sulkily; and then, with another voice, "But what matters hand of write?" he said. "I've seen him!"

"Seen him?" repeated Mr. Utterson. "Well?"

"That's it!" said Poole. "It was this way. I came suddenly into the theatre from the garden. It seems he had slipped out to look for this drug or whatever it is; for the cabinet door was open, and there he was at the far end of the room digging among the crates. He looked up when I came in, gave a kind of cry, and whipped upstairs into the cabinet. It was but for one minute that I saw him, but the hair stood upon my head like quills. Sir, if that was my master, why had he a mask upon his face? If it was my master, why did he cry out like a rat, and run from me? I have served him long enough. And then..." The man paused and passed his hand over his face.

"These are all very strange circumstances," said Mr. Utterson, "but I think I begin to see daylight. Your master, Poole, is plainly seized with one of those maladies that both torture and deform the sufferer; hence, for aught I know, the alteration of his voice; hence the mask and the avoidance of his friends; hence his eagerness to find this drug, by means of which the poor soul retains some hope of ultimate recovery—God grant that he be not deceived! There is my explanation; it is sad enough, Poole, ay, and appalling to consider; but it is plain and natural, hangs well together, and delivers us from all exorbitant alarms."

"Sir," said the butler, turning to a sort of mottled pallor, "that thing was not my master, and there's the truth. My master"—here he looked round him and began to whisper—"is a tall, fine build of a man, and this was more of a dwarf." Utterson attempted to protest. "O, sir," cried Poole, "do you think I do not know my master after twenty years? Do you think I do not know where his head comes to in the cabinet door, where I saw him every morning of my life? No, sir, that thing in the mask was never Dr. Jekyll—God knows what it was, but it was never Dr. Jekyll; and it is the belief of my heart that there was murder done."

"Poole," replied the lawyer, "if you say that, it will become my duty to make certain. Much as I desire to spare your master's feelings, much as I am puzzled by this note which seems to prove him to be still alive, I shall consider it my duty to break in that door."

"Ah, Mr. Utterson, that's talking!" cried the butler.

"And now comes the second question," resumed Utterson: "Who is going to do it?"

"Why, you and me, sir," was the undaunted reply.

"That's very well said," returned the lawyer; "and whatever comes of it, I shall make it my business to see you are no loser."

"There is an axe in the theatre," continued Poole; "and you might take the kitchen poker for yourself."

The lawyer took that rude but weighty instrument into his hand, and balanced it. "Do you know, Poole," he said, looking up, "that you and I are about to place ourselves in a position of some peril?"

"You may say so, sir, indeed," returned the butler.

"It is well, then that we should be frank," said the other. "We both think more than we have said; let us make a clean breast. This masked figure that you saw, did you recognise it?"

"Well, sir, it went so quick, and the creature was so doubled up, that I could hardly swear to that," was the answer. "But if you mean, was it Mr. Hyde?—why, yes, I think it was! You see, it was much of the same bigness; and it had the same quick, light way with it; and then who else could have got in by the laboratory door? You have not forgot, sir, that at the time of the murder he had still the key with him? But that's not all. I don't know, Mr. Utterson, if you ever met this Mr. Hyde?"

"Yes," said the lawyer, "I once spoke with him."

"Then you must know as well as the rest of us that there was something queer about that gentleman—something that gave a man a turn—I don't know rightly how to say it, sir, beyond this: that you felt in your marrow kind of cold and thin."

"I own I felt something of what you describe," said Mr. Utterson.

"Quite so, sir," returned Poole. "Well, when that masked thing like a monkey jumped from among the chemicals and whipped into the cabinet, it went down my spine like ice. O, I know it's not evidence, Mr. Utterson; I'm book-learned enough for that; but a man has his feelings, and I give you my bible-word it was Mr. Hyde!"

"Ay, ay," said the lawyer. "My fears incline to the same point. Evil, I fear, founded—evil was sure to come—of that connection. Ay truly, I believe you; I believe poor Harry is killed; and I believe his murderer (for what purpose, God alone can tell) is still lurking in his victim's room. Well, let our name be vengeance. Call Bradshaw."

> RLS uses Utterson to deflect the reader from coming close to the truth that Jekyll and Hyde are actually one and the same, even despite moving towards the end of the novella.

The footman came at the summons, very white and nervous.

"Pull yourself together, Bradshaw," said the lawyer. "This suspense, I know, is telling upon all of you; but it is now our intention to make an end of it. Poole, here, and I are going to force our way into the cabinet. If all is well, my shoulders are broad enough to bear the blame. Meanwhile, lest anything should really be amiss, or any malefactor seek to escape by the back, you and the boy must go round the corner with a pair of good sticks and take your post at the laboratory door. We give you ten minutes to get to your stations."

As Bradshaw left, the lawyer looked at his watch. "And now, Poole, let us get to ours," he said; and taking the poker under his arm, led the way into the yard. The scud had banked over the moon, and it was now quite dark. The wind, which only broke in puffs and draughts into that deep well of building, tossed the light of the candle to and fro about their steps, until they came into the shelter of the theatre, where they sat down silently to wait. London hummed solemnly all around; but nearer at hand, the stillness was only broken by the sounds of a footfall moving to and fro along the cabinet floor.

> 'scud' – cloud
>
> 'malefactor' – criminal
>
> An eerie atmosphere here in this paragraph. The repetition of 'to and fro' of the candlelight outside and the silent foot steps on the other side of the door.

"So it will walk all day, sir," whispered Poole; "ay, and the better part of the night. Only when a new sample comes from the chemist, there's a bit of a break. Ah, it's an ill conscience that's such an enemy to rest! Ah, sir, there's blood foully shed in every step of it! But hark again, a little closer—put your heart in your ears, Mr. Utterson, and tell me, is that the doctor's foot?"

The steps fell lightly and oddly, with a certain swing, for all they went so slowly; it was different indeed from the heavy creaking tread of Henry Jekyll. Utterson sighed. "Is there never anything else?" he asked.

Poole nodded. "Once," he said. "Once I heard it weeping!"

"Weeping? how that?" said the lawyer, conscious of a sudden chill of horror.

"Weeping like a woman or a lost soul," said the butler. "I came away with that upon my heart, that I could have wept too."

> To weep means to express grief and deepest sorrow. The horror comes from using the pronoun
>
> 'it' denoting something inhuman, undefinable, and therefore mysterious and evoking fear. 'It' denotes a monster, a beast, a fiend.
>
> All these sounds come from behind the locked door make them even more sinister – a locked door represents secrets, and something sinister.

But now the ten minutes drew to an end. Poole disinterred the axe from under a stack of packing straw; the candle was set upon the nearest table to light them to the attack; and they drew near with bated breath to where that patient foot was still going up and down, up and down, in the quiet of the night.

"Jekyll," cried Utterson, with a loud voice, "I demand to see you." He paused a moment, but there came no reply. "I give you fair warning, our suspicions are aroused, and I must and shall see you," he resumed; "if not by fair means, then by foul—if not of your consent, then by brute force!"

"Utterson," said the voice, "for God's sake, have mercy!"

"Ah, that's not Jekyll's voice—it's Hyde's!" cried Utterson. "Down with the door, Poole!"

Poole swung the axe over his shoulder; the blow shook the building, and the red baize door leaped against the lock and hinges.

> 'Red baize door' – the rising of the lower classes and breaking through the barriers set by wealth and class.

A dismal screech, as of mere animal terror, rang from the cabinet. Up went the axe again, and again the panels crashed and the frame bounded; four times the blow fell; but the wood was tough and the fittings were of excellent workmanship; and it was not until the fifth, that the lock burst and the wreck of the door fell inwards on the carpet.

The besiegers, appalled by their own riot and the stillness that had succeeded, stood back a little and peered in. There lay the cabinet before their eyes in the quiet lamplight, a good fire glowing and chattering on the hearth, the kettle singing its thin strain, a drawer or two open, papers neatly set forth on the business table, and nearer the fire, the things laid out for tea; the quietest room, you would have said, and, but for the glazed presses full of chemicals, the most commonplace that night in London.

> 'dismal screech' – dismal means dark, gloomy; screech means a scream like an animals.
>
> 'mere animal terror' – wild, in pain, agony, inhuman, not human,
>
> Contrast in a homely setting within, against the horror that was being felt by the servants, Poole and Utterson outside. Contrast also in the comfortable and cosy setting with the dead man on the floor.

Right in the middle there lay the body of a man sorely contorted and still twitching. They drew near on tiptoe, turned it on its back and beheld the face of Edward Hyde. He was dressed in clothes far too large for him, clothes of the doctor's bigness; the cords of his face still moved with a semblance of life, but life was quite gone; and by the crushed phial in the hand and the strong smell of kernels that hung upon the air, Utterson knew that he was looking on the body of a self-destroyer.

> Jekyll killed himself at the point where the door was broken, and at that same point, he was transitioning into Hyde. Hyde, desperate to live and be free of Jekyll would not have killed himself, so it was Jekyll who took the cyanide.
>
> 'self-destroyer' – suicide

"We have come too late," he said sternly, "whether to save or punish. Hyde is gone to his account; and it only remains for us to find the body of your master."

The far greater proportion of the building was occupied by the theatre, which filled almost the whole ground storey and was lighted from above, and by the cabinet, which formed an upper storey at one end and looked upon the court. A corridor joined the theatre to the door on the by-street; and with this the cabinet communicated separately by a second flight of stairs. There were besides a few dark closets and a spacious cellar. All these they now thoroughly examined. Each closet needed but a glance, for all were empty, and all, by the dust that fell from their doors, had stood long unopened. The cellar, indeed, was filled with crazy lumber, mostly dating from the times of the surgeon who was Jekyll's predecessor; but even as they opened the door they were advertised of the uselessness of further search, by the fall of a perfect mat of cobweb which had for years sealed up the entrance. Nowhere was there any trace of Henry Jekyll, dead or alive.

Poole stamped on the flags of the corridor. "He must be buried here," he said, hearkening to the sound.

"Or he may have fled," said Utterson, and he turned to examine the door in the by-street. It was locked; and lying near by on the flags, they found the key, already stained with rust.

"This does not look like use," observed the lawyer.

"Use!" echoed Poole. "Do you not see, sir, it is broken? much as if a man had stamped on it."

"Ay," continued Utterson, "and the fractures, too, are rusty." The two men looked at each other with a scare. "This is beyond me, Poole," said the lawyer. "Let us go back to the cabinet."

> 'Key' represents choice and control – the rusted and broken key means that Jekyll lost both these, and it was all of his own doing.
>
> Note the description of the house as being similar to Dr John Hunter's house as referenced in Addendum 2.

They mounted the stair in silence, and still with an occasional awestruck glance at the dead body, proceeded more thoroughly to examine the contents of the cabinet. At one table, there were traces of chemical work, various measured heaps of some white salt being laid on glass saucers, as though for an experiment in which the unhappy man had been prevented.

"That is the same drug that I was always bringing him," said Poole; and even as he spoke, the kettle with a startling noise boiled over.

This brought them to the fireside, where the easy-chair was drawn cosily up, and the tea things stood ready to the sitter's elbow, the very sugar in the cup. There were several books on a shelf; one lay beside the tea things open, and Utterson was amazed to find it a copy of a pious work, for which Jekyll had several times expressed a great esteem, annotated, in his own hand with startling blasphemies.

Next, in the course of their review of the chamber, the searchers came to the cheval-glass, into whose depths they looked with an involuntary horror. But it was so turned as to show them nothing but the rosy glow playing on the roof, the fire sparkling in a hundred repetitions along the glazed front of the presses, and their own pale and fearful countenances stooping to look in.

"This glass has seen some strange things, sir," whispered Poole.

---

The cheval glass is turned up towards the roof. This is a very odd position. Since the primary theme is the hypocrisy of the middle-class gentleman and since these gentlemen are the amongst the readership, the glass is turned upwards towards them.

'Mirror' connotes reflection, truth, awareness.

Breaking the door did not in fact solve the case. Utterson introduces more mystery by referencing that Jekyll is nowhere to be found. This maintains the momentum of the mystery and tension and fear.

---

"And surely none stranger than itself," echoed the lawyer in the same tones. "For what did Jekyll"—he caught himself up at the word with a start, and then conquering the weakness—"what could Jekyll want with it?" he said.

"You may say that!" said Poole.

Next they turned to the business table. On the desk, among the neat array of papers, a large envelope was uppermost, and bore, in the doctor's hand, the name of Mr. Utterson. The lawyer unsealed it, and several enclosures fell to the floor. The first was a will, drawn in the same eccentric terms as the one which he had returned six months before, to serve as a testament in case of death and as a deed of gift in case of disappearance; but in place of the name of Edward Hyde, the lawyer, with indescribable amazement read the name of Gabriel John Utterson. He looked at Poole, and then back at the paper, and last of all at the dead malefactor stretched upon the carpet.

"My head goes round," he said. "He has been all these days in possession; he had no cause to like me; he must have raged to see himself displaced; and he has not destroyed this document."

He caught up the next paper; it was a brief note in the doctor's hand and dated at the top. "O Poole!" the lawyer cried, "he was alive and here this day. He cannot have been disposed of in so short a space; he must be still alive, he must have fled! And then, why fled? and how? and in that case, can we venture to declare this suicide? O, we must be careful. I foresee that we may yet involve your master in some dire catastrophe."

"Why don't you read it, sir?" asked Poole.

"Because I fear," replied the lawyer solemnly. "God grant I have no cause for it!" And with that he brought the paper to his eyes and read as follows:

"My dear Utterson,—When this shall fall into your hands, I shall have disappeared, under what circumstances I have not the penetration to foresee, but my instinct and all the circumstances of my nameless situation tell me that the end is sure and must be early. Go then, and first read the narrative which Lanyon warned me he was to place in your hands; and if you care to hear more, turn to the confession of

"Your unworthy and unhappy friend,

"HENRY JEKYLL."

"There was a third enclosure?" asked Utterson.

"Here, sir," said Poole, and gave into his hands a considerable packet sealed in several places.

The lawyer put it in his pocket. "I would say nothing of this paper. If your master has fled or is dead, we may at least save his credit. It is now ten; I must go home and read these documents in quiet; but I shall be back before midnight, when we shall send for the police."

They went out, locking the door of the theatre behind them; and Utterson, once more leaving the servants gathered about the fire in the hall, trudged back to his office to read the two narratives in which this mystery was now to be explained.

## 9: Dr. Lanyon's Narrative

On the ninth of January, now four days ago, I received by the evening delivery a registered envelope, addressed in the hand of my colleague and old school companion, Henry Jekyll. I was a good deal surprised by this; for we were by no means in the habit of correspondence; I had seen the man, dined with him, indeed, the night before; and I could imagine nothing in our intercourse that should justify formality of registration. The contents increased my wonder; for this is how the letter ran:

"10$^{th}$ December, 18—.

"Dear Lanyon,—You are one of my oldest friends; and although we may have differed at times on scientific questions, I cannot remember, at least on my side, any break in our affection. There was never a day when, if you had said to me, 'Jekyll, my life, my honour, my reason, depend upon you,' I would not have sacrificed my left hand to help you. Lanyon, my life, my honour, my reason, are all at your mercy; if you fail me to-night, I am lost. You might suppose, after this preface, that I am going to ask you for something dishonourable to grant. Judge for yourself.

> The dates are hazy. Jekyll's letter to Lanyon is dated the 10th December. They all dined together on the 8th January. Lanyon receives the letter on the 9th January which was four days ago, so this night should be the 13th January. Explanation given in Appendix A.
>
> Clearly, Jekyll's letter to Lanyon is at odds with his opinion of hm as being a 'hide bound pedant'. To argue that Jekyll is good, is incorrect, if we look at this act. He dislikes Lanyon, then proceeds to almost teach Lanyon a lesson.

"I want you to postpone all other engagements for to-night—ay, even if you were summoned to the bedside of an emperor; to take a cab, unless your carriage should be actually at the door; and with this letter in your hand for consultation, to drive straight to my house. Poole, my butler, has his orders; you will find him waiting your arrival with a locksmith. The door of my cabinet is then to be forced; and you are to go in alone; to open the glazed press (letter E) on the left hand, breaking the lock if it be shut; and to draw out, *with all its contents as they stand*, the fourth drawer from the top or (which is the same thing) the third from the bottom. In my extreme distress of mind, I have a morbid fear of misdirecting you; but even if I am in error, you may know the right drawer by its contents: some powders, a phial and a paper book. This drawer I beg of you to carry back with you to Cavendish Square exactly as it stands.

"That is the first part of the service: now for the second. You should be back, if you set out at once on the receipt of this, long before midnight; but I will leave you that amount of margin, not only in the fear of one of those obstacles that can neither be prevented nor foreseen, but because an hour when your servants are in bed is to be preferred for what will then remain to do. At midnight, then, I have to ask you to be alone in your consulting room, to admit with your own hand into the house a man who will present himself in my name, and to place in his hands the drawer that you will have brought with you from my cabinet. Then you will have played your part and earned my gratitude completely. Five minutes afterwards, if you insist upon an explanation, you will have understood that these arrangements are of capital importance; and that by the neglect of one of them, fantastic as they must appear, you might have charged your conscience with my death or the shipwreck of my reason.

"Confident as I am that you will not trifle with this appeal, my heart sinks and my hand trembles at the bare thought of such a possibility. Think of me at this hour, in a strange place, labouring under a blackness of distress that no fancy can exaggerate, and yet well aware that, if you will but punctually serve me, my troubles will roll away like a story that is told. Serve me, my dear Lanyon and save

"Your friend,

"H.J.

"P.S.—I had already sealed this up when a fresh terror struck upon my soul. It is possible that the post-office may fail me, and this letter not come into your hands until to-morrow morning. In that case, dear Lanyon, do my errand when it shall be most convenient for you in the course of the day; and once more expect my messenger at midnight. It may then already be too late; and if that night passes without event, you will know that you have seen the last of Henry Jekyll."

Upon the reading of this letter, I made sure my colleague was insane; but till that was proved beyond the possibility of doubt, I felt bound to do as he requested. The less I understood of this farrago, the less I was in a position to judge of its importance; and an appeal so worded could not be set aside without a grave responsibility. I rose accordingly from table, got into a hansom, and drove straight to Jekyll's house. The butler was awaiting my arrival; he had received by the same post as mine a registered letter of instruction, and had sent at once for a locksmith and a carpenter. The tradesmen came while we were yet speaking; and we moved in a body to old Dr. Denman's surgical theatre, from which (as you are doubtless aware) Jekyll's private cabinet is most conveniently entered. The door was very strong, the lock excellent; the carpenter avowed he would have great trouble and have to do much damage, if force were to be used; and the locksmith was near despair. But this last was a handy fellow, and after two hour's work, the door stood open. The press marked E was unlocked; and I took out the drawer, had it filled up with straw and tied in a sheet, and returned with it to Cavendish Square.

Here I proceeded to examine its contents. The powders were neatly enough made up, but not with the nicety of the dispensing chemist; so that it was plain they were of Jekyll's private manufacture; and when I opened one of the wrappers I found what seemed to me a simple crystalline salt of a white colour. The phial, to which I next turned my attention, might have been about half full of a blood-red liquor, which was highly pungent to the sense of smell and seemed to me to contain phosphorus and some volatile ether. At the other ingredients I could make no guess. The book was an ordinary version book and contained little but a series of dates. These covered a period of many years, but I observed that the entries ceased nearly a year ago and quite abruptly. Here and there a brief remark was appended to a date, usually no more than a single word: "double" occurring perhaps six times in a total of several hundred entries; and once very early in the list and followed by several marks of exclamation, "total failure!!!" All this, though it whetted my curiosity, told me little that was definite. Here were a phial of some salt, and the record of a series of experiments that had led (like too many of Jekyll's investigations) to no end of practical usefulness. How could the presence of these articles in my house affect either the honour, the sanity, or the life of my flighty colleague? If his messenger could go to one place, why could he not go to another? And even granting some impediment, why was this gentleman to be received by me in secret? The more I reflected the more convinced I grew that I was dealing with a case of cerebral disease; and though I dismissed my servants to bed, I loaded an old revolver, that I might be found in some posture of self-defence.

Twelve o'clock had scarce rung out over London, ere the knocker sounded very gently on the door. I went myself at the summons, and found a small man crouching against the pillars of the portico.

"Are you come from Dr. Jekyll?" I asked.

He told me "yes" by a constrained gesture; and when I had bidden him enter, he did not obey me without a searching backward glance into the darkness of the square. There was a policeman not far off, advancing with his bull's eye open; and at the sight, I thought my visitor started and made greater haste.

These particulars struck me, I confess, disagreeably; and as I followed him into the bright light of the consulting room, I kept my hand ready on my weapon. Here, at last, I had a chance of clearly seeing him. I had never set eyes on him before, so much was certain. He was small, as I have said; I was struck besides with the shocking expression of his face, with his remarkable combination of great muscular activity and great apparent debility of constitution, and—last but not least—with the odd, subjective disturbance caused by his neighbourhood. This bore some resemblance to incipient rigour, and was accompanied by a marked sinking of the pulse. At the time, I set it down to some idiosyncratic, personal distaste, and merely wondered at the acuteness of the symptoms; but I have since had reason to believe the cause to lie much deeper in the nature of man, and to turn on some nobler hinge than the principle of hatred.

'Incipient' – the beginnings of

'Misbegotten' – something deformed or detestable.

Dr Lanyon is trying to explain his physical symptoms of being in the presence of Hyde in a rational and logical way.

This person (who had thus, from the first moment of his entrance, struck in me what I can only describe as a disgustful curiosity) was dressed in a fashion that would have made an ordinary person laughable; his clothes, that is to say, although they were of rich and sober fabric, were enormously too large for him in every measurement—the trousers hanging on his legs and rolled up to keep them from the ground, the waist of the coat below his haunches, and the collar sprawling wide upon his shoulders. Strange to relate, this ludicrous accoutrement was far from moving me to laughter. Rather, as there was something abnormal and misbegotten in the very essence of the creature that now faced me—something seizing, surprising and revolting—this fresh disparity seemed but to fit in with and to reinforce it; so that to my interest in the man's nature and character, there was added a curiosity as to his origin, his life, his fortune and status in the world.

Hyde wears the clothes of Dr Jekyll. The sight of this is both abnormal and revolting because it is the low-class looking Hyde wearing high class clothes.

These observations, though they have taken so great a space to be set down in, were yet the work of a few seconds. My visitor was, indeed, on fire with sombre excitement.

"Have you got it?" he cried. "Have you got it?" And so lively was his impatience that he even laid his hand upon my arm and sought to shake me.

Hyde behaves in a bestial and uncontrolled manner. He is unpredictable.

92

I put him back, conscious at his touch of a certain icy pang along my blood. "Come, sir," said I. "You forget that I have not yet the pleasure of your acquaintance. Be seated, if you please." And I showed him an example, and sat down myself in my customary seat and with as fair an imitation of my ordinary manner to a patient, as the lateness of the hour, the nature of my preoccupations, and the horror I had of my visitor, would suffer me to muster.

"I beg your pardon, Dr. Lanyon," he replied civilly enough. "What you say is very well founded; and my impatience has shown its heels to my politeness. I come here at the instance of your colleague, Dr. Henry Jekyll, on a piece of business of some moment; and I understood..." He paused and put his hand to his throat, and I could see, in spite of his collected manner, that he was wrestling against the approaches of the hysteria—"I understood, a drawer..."

But here I took pity on my visitor's suspense, and some perhaps on my own growing curiosity.

"There it is, sir," said I, pointing to the drawer, where it lay on the floor behind a table and still covered with the sheet.

He sprang to it, and then paused, and laid his hand upon his heart; I could hear his teeth grate with the convulsive action of his jaws; and his face was so ghastly to see that I grew alarmed both for his life and reason.

"Compose yourself," said I.

He turned a dreadful smile to me, and as if with the decision of despair, plucked away the sheet. At sight of the contents, he uttered one loud sob of such immense relief that I sat petrified. And the next moment, in a voice that was already fairly well under control, "Have you a graduated glass?" he asked.

I rose from my place with something of an effort and gave him what he asked.

He thanked me with a smiling nod, measured out a few minims of the red tincture and added one of the powders. The mixture, which was at first of a reddish hue, began, in proportion as the crystals melted, to brighten in colour, to effervesce audibly, and to throw off small fumes of vapour. Suddenly and at the same moment, the ebullition ceased and the compound changed to a dark purple, which faded again more slowly to a watery green. My visitor, who had watched these metamorphoses with a keen eye, smiled, set down the glass upon the table, and then turned and looked upon me with an air of scrutiny.

> The Victorian era was a time of great scientific advancement. Ironically, it fed the imagination in terms of the power and mystery and magic that came from it. Of course, science and technology is none of these things, it is facts and figures and cause and effect.

"And now," said he, "to settle what remains. Will you be wise? will you be guided? will you suffer me to take this glass in my hand and to go forth from your house without further parley? or has the greed of curiosity too much command of you? Think before you answer, for it shall be done as you decide. As you decide, you shall be left as you were before, and neither richer nor wiser, unless the sense of service rendered to a man in mortal distress may be counted as a kind of riches of the soul. Or, if you shall so prefer to choose, a new province of knowledge and new avenues to fame and power shall be laid open to you, here, in this room, upon the instant; and your sight shall be blasted by a prodigy to stagger the unbelief of Satan."

> The primary readership for this novella are the MCM. The lower classes are at this time wholly illiterate. Therefore, when Hyde asks Lanyon the above questions, he is also asking the same of the MCM reader. The narrative extends to the reader.
>
> Many people in Victorian England were afraid that scientific advances went against religious teachings, so Darwin's theory flew in the face of Creationism and Adam and Eze.
>
> Therefore, the use of rhetorical questions towards Lanyon extend beyond the text towards the reader.
>
> Repetition of 'prodigy' – this hints that there is a relationship between Jekyll and Hyde.

"Sir," said I, affecting a coolness that I was far from truly possessing, "you speak enigmas, and you will perhaps not wonder that I hear you with no very strong impression of belief. But I have gone too far in the way of inexplicable services to pause before I see the end."

"It is well," replied my visitor. "Lanyon, you remember your vows: what follows is under the seal of our profession. And now, you who have so long been bound to the most narrow and material views, you who have denied the virtue of transcendental medicine, you who have derided your superiors—behold!"

> 'Your vows and our professional seal' – he refers to the Hippocratic oath.
>
> Hyde betrays himself in the use of the personal pronoun, 'our profession'. Hyde is a Mr not a Dr.

He put the glass to his lips and drank at one gulp. A cry followed; he reeled, staggered, clutched at the table and held on, staring with injected eyes, gasping with open mouth; and as I looked there came, I thought, a change—he seemed to swell—his face became suddenly black and the features seemed to melt and alter—and the next moment, I had sprung to my feet and leaped back against the wall, my arms raised to shield me from that prodigy, my mind submerged in terror.

"O God!" I screamed, and "O God!" again and again; for there before my eyes—pale and shaken, and half fainting, and groping before him with his hands, like a man restored from death—there stood Henry Jekyll!

> It is testament to Stevenson's art as a storyteller that we only now learn, at the very end of his novella that Jekyll IS Hyde.
>
> This secret locked away, in the dead Dr Lanyon, in his letter read posthumously, and now only being read by the secretive Utterson may never come to light.

What he told me in the next hour, I cannot bring my mind to set on paper. I saw what I saw, I heard what I heard, and my soul sickened at it; and yet now when that sight has faded from my eyes, I ask myself if I believe it, and I cannot answer. My life is shaken to its roots; sleep has left me; the deadliest terror sits by me at all hours of the day and night; and I feel that my days are numbered, and that I must die; and yet I shall die incredulous. As for the moral turpitude that man unveiled to me, even with tears of penitence, I cannot, even in memory, dwell on it without a start of horror. I will say but one thing, Utterson, and that (if you can bring your mind to credit it) will be more than enough. The creature who crept into my house that night was, on Jekyll's own confession, known by the name of Hyde and hunted for in every corner of the land as the murderer of Carew.

HASTIE LANYON.

> Dr Lanyon, witnessing the horror that is Hyde and then the horror that is Jekyll transmogrifying before his very eyes is enough to send him to his death. He is the only character to witness the change.

## 10: Henry Jekyll's Full Statement of the Case

I was born in the year 18— to a large fortune, endowed besides with excellent parts, inclined by nature to industry, fond of the respect of the wise and good among my fellowmen, and thus, as might have been supposed, with every guarantee of an honourable and distinguished future. And indeed the worst of my faults was a certain impatient gaiety of disposition, such as has made the happiness of many, but such as I found it hard to reconcile with my imperious desire to carry my head high, and wear a more than commonly grave countenance before the public.

> Jekyll likes to enjoy himself, just like many others. However, the problem is he still wants to hold his head up high. Therefore, he wants a clean reputation. He is therefore conflicted and split but not by his good and bad nature, but by reputation. Reputation is how he appears in front of his peers, his fellow MCM. Therefore, it is societal restrictions which prevent him from indulging his desires openly. Society respects good or those who appear good.
>
> Therefore, it follows that if society lets the minor aberrations pass, then the more serious ones can be avoided possibly.
>
> In any question, you must challenge the concept that Jekyll is GOOD. He is not. He was doing all the things that Hyde was doing before he discovered the potion. Hyde came into being to protect Jekyll's REPUTATION.

Hence it came about that I concealed my pleasures; and that when I reached years of reflection, and began to look round me and take stock of my progress and position in the world, I stood already committed to a profound duplicity of life.

> The word 'duplicity' shows that Jekyll believed that he was living a lie.

Many a man would have even blazoned such irregularities as I was guilty of; but from the high views that I had set before me, I regarded and hid them with an almost morbid sense of shame. It was thus rather the exacting nature of my aspirations than any particular degradation in my faults, that made me what I was, and, with even a deeper trench than in the majority of men, severed in me those provinces of good and ill which divide and compound man's dual nature. In this case, I was driven to reflect deeply and inveterately on that hard law of life, which lies at the root of religion and is one of the most plentiful springs of distress.

---

'blazoned' – display, exhibited.

'irregularities' – improper and dishonest behaviour.

There is a conflict between following one's own desires and those of God. Desire and restraint. Public and private life.

'hard law of life…root of religion' – original sin that must be repressed completely. He is distressed because he enjoys being bad but religion says that you cannot be bad.

---

Though so profound a double-dealer, I was in no sense a hypocrite; both sides of me were in dead earnest; I was no more myself when I laid aside restraint and plunged in shame, than when I laboured, in the eye of day, at the furtherance of knowledge or the relief of sorrow and suffering. And it chanced that the direction of my scientific studies, which led wholly towards the mystic and the transcendental, reacted and shed a strong light on this consciousness of the perennial war among my members. With every day, and from both sides of my intelligence, the moral and the intellectual, I thus drew steadily nearer to that truth, by whose partial discovery I have been doomed to such a dreadful shipwreck: that man is not truly one, but truly two. I say two, because the state of my own knowledge does not pass beyond that point. Others will follow, others will outstrip me on the same lines; and I hazard the guess that man will be ultimately known for a mere polity of multifarious, incongruous and independent denizens. I, for my part, from the nature of my life, advanced infallibly in one direction and in one direction only. It was on the moral side, and in my own person, that I learned to recognise the thorough and primitive duality of man; I saw that, of the two natures that contended in the field of my consciousness, even if I could rightly be said to be either, it was only because I was radically both; and from an early date, even before the course of my scientific discoveries had begun to suggest the most naked possibility of such a miracle, I had learned to dwell with pleasure, as a beloved daydream, on the thought of the separation of these elements. If each, I told myself, could be housed in separate identities, life would be relieved of all that was unbearable; the unjust might go his way, delivered from the aspirations and remorse of his more upright twin; and the just could walk steadfastly and securely on his upward path, doing the good things in which he found his pleasure, and no longer exposed to disgrace and penitence by the hands of this extraneous evil. It was the curse of mankind that these incongruous faggots were thus bound together—that in the agonised womb of consciousness, these polar twins should be continuously struggling. How, then were they dissociated?

---

'in no sense a hypocrite' – as the MCM all are.

'man will be ultimately known for a mere polity of multifarious, incongruous and independent denizens' – a society of diverse, good and bad, disharmonious individuals.

'mystic and transcendental' – supernatural, demonic.

---

'in no sense a hypocrite' – as the MCM all are.

'man will be ultimately known for a mere polity of multifarious, incongruous and independent denizens' – a society of diverse, good and bad, disharmonious individuals.

'mystic and transcendental' – supernatural, demonic.

'Incongruous' means odd, strange, incompatible.

'Faggots' – bundle of sticks, for burning, firewood.

'disassociate' – disconnect.

He wants to the separate good and evil in separate bodies.

'agonised womb' 'polar twins' – this is from the beginning, pre-birth. It is not nurture, it is nature.

I was so far in my reflections when, as I have said, a side light began to shine upon the subject from the laboratory table. I began to perceive more deeply than it has ever yet been stated, the trembling immateriality, the mistlike transience, of this seemingly so solid body in which we walk attired. Certain agents I found to have the power to shake and pluck back that fleshly vestment, even as a wind might toss the curtains of a pavilion. For two good reasons, I will not enter deeply into this scientific branch of my confession. First, because I have been made to learn that the doom and burthen of our life is bound for ever on man's shoulders, and when the attempt is made to cast it off, it but returns upon us with more unfamiliar and more awful pressure. Second, because, as my narrative will make, alas! too evident, my discoveries were incomplete. Enough then, that I not only recognised my natural body from the mere aura and effulgence of certain of the powers that made up my spirit, but managed to compound a drug by which these powers should be dethroned from their supremacy, and a second form and countenance substituted, none the less natural to me because they were the expression, and bore the stamp of lower elements in my soul.

'immateriality, the mistlike transience, of this seemingly so solid body in which we walk attired' – acting like God, trying to change the body. Taking charge of the human body and the soul which is a divine thing given by God.

'fleshly vestment' – human body.

'aura' – a concept from Spiritualism (Not Christianity) that means some part of the individual that emanates from them like light. Jekyll is referring to the Soul, which is divine but is contrasting this against a term of spiritualism which is partly pagan.

'dethroned from their supremacy' and 'lower elements of my soul' – Jekyll defying God by playing with the immortal Soul.

'effulgence' – the ability to shine brightly.

I hesitated long before I put this theory to the test of practice. I knew well that I risked death; for any drug that so potently controlled and shook the very fortress of identity, might, by the least scruple of an overdose or at the least inopportunity in the moment of exhibition, utterly blot out that immaterial tabernacle which I looked to it to change. But the temptation of a discovery so singular and profound at last overcame the suggestions of alarm. I had long since prepared my tincture; I purchased at once, from a firm of wholesale chemists, a large quantity of a particular salt which I knew, from my experiments, to be the last ingredient required; and late one accursed night, I compounded the elements, watched them boil and smoke together in the glass, and when the ebullition had subsided, with a strong glow of courage, drank off the potion.

'fortress of identity' – the physical body, reputation.

This 'late one night' is very reminiscent of Frankenstein and the bringing of the monster to life. It is deeply fitting that these two monsters of the Gothic genre came into being from the real nightmares of their creators. Both Mary Shelley and RLS conceived their novels by having terrifying dreams, Shelley dreamt that she saw a student leaning over the creature he had created and its eyes fluttered open and RLS dreamt about Jekyll transforming into Hyde.

'immaterial tabernacle' – the soul.

The most racking pangs succeeded: a grinding in the bones, deadly nausea, and a horror of the spirit that cannot be exceeded at the hour of birth or death. Then these agonies began swiftly to subside, and I came to myself as if out of a great sickness. There was something strange in my sensations, something indescribably new and, from its very novelty, incredibly sweet. I felt younger, lighter, happier in body; within I was conscious of a heady recklessness, a current of disordered sensual images running like a millrace in my fancy, a solution of the bonds of obligation, an unknown but not an innocent freedom of the soul. I knew myself, at the first breath of this new life, to be more wicked, tenfold more wicked, sold a slave to my original evil; and the thought, in that moment, braced and delighted me like wine. I stretched out my hands, exulting in the freshness of these sensations; and in the act, I was suddenly aware that I had lost in stature.

Jekyll's change into Hyde is not unlike the act of childbirth, and the child that is born is the shorter, smaller Hyde.

'delighted me like wine' – another connection here between immorality and being intoxicated.

There was no mirror, at that date, in my room; that which stands beside me as I write, was brought there later on and for the very purpose of these transformations. The night however, was far gone into the morning—the morning, black as it was, was nearly ripe for the conception of the day—the inmates of my house were locked in the most rigorous hours of slumber; and I determined, flushed as I was with hope and triumph, to venture in my new shape as far as to my bedroom. I crossed the yard, wherein the constellations looked down upon me, I could have thought, with wonder, the first creature of that sort that their unsleeping vigilance had yet disclosed to them; I stole through the corridors, a stranger in my own house; and coming to my room, I saw for the first time the appearance of Edward Hyde.

I must here speak by theory alone, saying not that which I know, but that which I suppose to be most probable. The evil side of my nature, to which I had now transferred the stamping efficacy, was less robust and less developed than the good which I had just deposed. Again, in the course of my life, which had been, after all, nine tenths a life of effort, virtue and control, it had been much less exercised and much less exhausted.

And hence, as I think, it came about that Edward Hyde was so much smaller, slighter and younger than Henry Jekyll. Even as good shone upon the countenance of the one, evil was written broadly and plainly on the face of the other. Evil besides (which I must still believe to be the lethal side of man) had left on that body an imprint of deformity and decay. And yet when I looked upon that ugly idol in the glass, I was conscious of no repugnance, rather of a leap of welcome. This, too, was myself. It seemed natural and human. In my eyes it bore a livelier image of the spirit, it seemed more express and single, than the imperfect and divided countenance I had been hitherto accustomed to call mine. And in so far I was doubtless right. I have observed that when I wore the semblance of Edward Hyde, none could come near to me at first without a visible misgiving of the flesh. This, as I take it, was because all human beings, as we meet them, are commingled out of good and evil: and Edward Hyde, alone in the ranks of mankind, was pure evil.

I lingered but a moment at the mirror: the second and conclusive experiment had yet to be attempted; it yet remained to be seen if I had lost my identity beyond redemption and must flee before daylight from a house that was no longer mine; and hurrying back to my cabinet, I once more prepared and drank the cup, once more suffered the pangs of dissolution, and came to myself once more with the character, the stature and the face of Henry Jekyll.

That night I had come to the fatal cross-roads. Had I approached my discovery in a more noble spirit, had I risked the experiment while under the empire of generous or pious aspirations, all must have been otherwise, and from these agonies of death and birth, I had come forth an angel instead of a fiend. The drug had no discriminating action; it was neither diabolical nor divine; it but shook the doors of the prisonhouse of my disposition; and like the captives of Philippi, that which stood within ran forth. At that time my virtue slumbered; my evil, kept awake by ambition, was alert and swift to seize the occasion; and the thing that was projected was Edward Hyde. Hence, although I had now two characters as well as two appearances, one was wholly evil, and the other was still the old Henry Jekyll, that incongruous compound of whose reformation and improvement I had already learned to despair. The movement was thus wholly toward the worse.

Even at that time, I had not conquered my aversions to the dryness of a life of study. I would still be merrily disposed at times; and as my pleasures were (to say the least) undignified, and I was not only well known and highly considered, but growing towards the elderly man, this incoherency of my life was daily growing more unwelcome. It was on this side that my new power tempted me until I fell in slavery. I had but to drink the cup, to doff at once the body of the noted professor, and to assume, like a thick cloak, that of Edward Hyde. I smiled at the notion; it seemed to me at the time to be humourous; and I made my preparations with the most studious care. I took and furnished that house in Soho, to which Hyde was tracked by the police; and engaged as a housekeeper a creature whom I knew well to be silent and unscrupulous. On the other side, I announced to my servants that a Mr. Hyde (whom I described) was to have full liberty and power about my house in the square; and to parry mishaps, I even called and made myself a familiar object, in my second character. I next drew up that will to which you so much objected; so that if anything befell me in the person of Dr. Jekyll, I could enter on that of Edward Hyde without pecuniary loss. And thus fortified, as I supposed, on every side, I began to profit by the strange immunities of my position.

Men have before hired bravos to transact their crimes, while their own person and reputation sat under shelter. I was the first that ever did so for his pleasures. I was the first that could plod in the public eye with a load of genial respectability, and in a moment, like a schoolboy, strip off these lendings and spring headlong into the sea of liberty. But for me, in my impenetrable mantle, the safety was complete. Think of it—I did not even exist! Let me but escape into my laboratory door, give me but a second or two to mix and swallow the draught that I had always standing ready; and whatever he had done, Edward Hyde would pass away like the stain of breath upon a mirror; and there in his stead, quietly at home, trimming the midnight lamp in his study, a man who could afford to laugh at suspicion, would be Henry Jekyll.

The pleasures which I made haste to seek in my disguise were, as I have said, undignified; I would scarce use a harder term. But in the hands of Edward Hyde, they soon began to turn toward the monstrous. When I would come back from these excursions, I was often plunged into a kind of wonder at my vicarious depravity.

Any student must take the fact that Jekyll represents 'good' with a pinch of salt. If he were good, he would be disgusted and appalled by the acts of Hyde, but he admires them.

Vladimir Nabokov's lecture on Strange Case of Dr Jekyll and Mr Hyde

From "Lectures on Literature"*.he states that:

"Is Jekyll good? No, he is a composite being, a mixture of good and bad, a preparation consisting of a 99% solution of Jekyllite and 1% of Hyde [...] Jekyll's morals are poor from the Victorian point of view. He is a hypocritical creature carefully concealing his little sins. He is vindictive, never forgiving Dr Lanyon with whom he disagrees in scientific matters. He is foolhardy. Hyde is mingled with him, within him."

Therefore, do challenge the idea that Jekyll is wholly good.

This familiar that I called out of my own soul, and sent forth alone to do his good pleasure, was a being inherently malign and villainous; his every act and thought centered on self; drinking pleasure with bestial avidity from any degree of torture to another; relentless like a man of stone. Henry Jekyll stood at times aghast before the acts of Edward Hyde; but the situation was apart from ordinary laws, and insidiously relaxed the grasp of conscience. It was Hyde, after all, and Hyde alone, that was guilty. Jekyll was no worse; he woke again to his good qualities seemingly unimpaired; he would even make haste, where it was possible, to undo the evil done by Hyde. And thus his conscience slumbered.

Note the absence of any detail. We have no idea as to the immoralities or depraved behaviour that Hyde commits. However, we must always bear in mind that Hyde is not a separate entity. He is merely a mask, a cover up for Jekyll. By distancing himself from Hyde, he can also distance himself from all that Hyde does and therefore from guilt; we only feel guilty when we do something wrong.

'drinking pleasure with bestial avidity from any degree of torture to another' – connection to alcohol, getting pleasure from the pain of others. 'bestial' connotes beast, wild, feral.

Into the details of the infamy at which I thus connived (for even now I can scarce grant that I committed it) I have no design of entering; I mean but to point out the warnings and the successive steps with which my chastisement approached. I met with one accident which, as it brought on no consequence, I shall no more than mention. An act of cruelty to a child aroused against me the anger of a passer-by, whom I recognised the other day in the person of your kinsman; the doctor and the child's family joined him; there were moments when I feared for my life; and at last, in order to pacify their too just resentment, Edward Hyde had to bring them to the door, and pay them in a cheque drawn in the name of Henry Jekyll. But this danger was easily eliminated from the future, by opening an account at another bank in the name of Edward Hyde himself; and when, by sloping my own hand backward, I had supplied my double with a signature, I thought I sat beyond the reach of fate.

We arrive now at the start of the novella, the incident of the door and the poor little girl. He pays no mind to the distress caused to the little girl, rather he learns the lesson that opens a new bank account in the name of Edward Hyde.

Some two months before the murder of Sir Danvers, I had been out for one of my adventures, had returned at a late hour, and woke the next day in bed with somewhat odd sensations. It was in vain I looked about me; in vain I saw the decent furniture and tall proportions of my room in the square; in vain that I recognised the pattern of the bed curtains and the design of the mahogany frame; something still kept insisting that I was not where I was, that I had not wakened where I seemed to be, but in the little room in Soho where I was accustomed to sleep in the body of Edward Hyde. I smiled to myself, and in my psychological way, began lazily to inquire into the elements of this illusion, occasionally, even as I did so, dropping back into a comfortable morning doze. I was still so engaged when, in one of my more wakeful moments, my eyes fell upon my hand. Now the hand of Henry Jekyll (as you have often remarked) was professional in shape and size; it was large, firm, white and comely. But the hand which I now saw, clearly enough, in the yellow light of a mid-London morning, lying half shut on the bedclothes, was lean, corded, knuckly, of a dusky pallor and thickly shaded with a swart growth of hair. It was the hand of Edward Hyde.

> This is the first time that things start to go wrong for Jekyll. He has gone to bed as Jekyll, in Cavendish Square, but when he awakes, his hand is that of Hyde. His consciousness however betrays himself to be that of Jekyll. He writes and reacts as Jekyll whilst in Hyde's body.

I must have stared upon it for near half a minute, sunk as I was in the mere stupidity of wonder, before terror woke up in my breast as sudden and startling as the crash of cymbals; and bounding from my bed I rushed to the mirror. At the sight that met my eyes, my blood was changed into something exquisitely thin and icy. Yes, I had gone to bed Henry Jekyll, I had awakened Edward Hyde. How was this to be explained? I asked myself; and then, with another bound of terror—how was it to be remedied? It was well on in the morning; the servants were up; all my drugs were in the cabinet—a long journey down two pairs of stairs, through the back passage, across the open court and through the anatomical theatre, from where I was then standing horror-struck. It might indeed be possible to cover my face; but of what use was that, when I was unable to conceal the alteration in my stature? And then with an overpowering sweetness of relief, it came back upon my mind that the servants were already used to the coming and going of my second self. I had soon dressed, as well as I was able, in clothes of my own size: had soon passed through the house, where Bradshaw stared and drew back at seeing Mr. Hyde at such an hour and in such a strange array; and ten minutes later, Dr. Jekyll had returned to his own shape and was sitting down, with a darkened brow, to make a feint of breakfasting.

Small indeed was my appetite. This inexplicable incident, this reversal of my previous experience, seemed, like the Babylonian finger on the wall, to be spelling out the letters of my judgment; and I began to reflect more seriously than ever before on the issues and possibilities of my double existence. That part of me which I had the power of projecting, had lately been much exercised and nourished; it had seemed to me of late as though the body of Edward Hyde had grown in stature, as though (when I wore that form) I were conscious of a more generous tide of blood; and I began to spy a danger that, if this were much prolonged, the balance of my nature might be permanently overthrown, the power of voluntary change be forfeited, and the character of Edward Hyde become irrevocably mine. The power of the drug had not been always equally displayed. Once, very early in my career, it had totally failed me; since then I had been obliged on more than one occasion to double, and once, with infinite risk of death, to treble the amount; and these rare uncertainties had cast hitherto the sole shadow on my contentment. Now, however, and in the light of that morning's accident, I was led to remark that whereas, in the beginning, the difficulty had been to throw off the body of Jekyll, it had of late gradually but decidedly transferred itself to the other side. All things therefore seemed to point to this; that I was slowly losing hold of my original and better self, and becoming slowly incorporated with my second and worse.

> Babylonian finger on the wall – writing on the wall appearing to Daniel prophesying the end of King Belshazzar; foreshadowing through the use of Biblical allusion.
>
> Jekyll realises that Hyde is growing in size, the transformative power of the drug is wavering, and at the last, Jekyll is losing control.

Between these two, I now felt I had to choose. My two natures had memory in common, but all other faculties were most unequally shared between them. Jekyll (who was composite) now with the most sensitive apprehensions, now with a greedy gusto, projected and shared in the pleasures and adventures of Hyde; but Hyde was indifferent to Jekyll, or but remembered him as the mountain bandit remembers the cavern in which he conceals himself from pursuit. Jekyll had more than a father's interest; Hyde had more than a son's indifference. To cast in my lot with Jekyll, was to die to those appetites which I had long secretly indulged and had of late begun to pamper. To cast it in with Hyde, was to die to a thousand interests and aspirations, and to become, at a blow and forever, despised and friendless. The bargain might appear unequal; but there was still another consideration in the scales; for while Jekyll would suffer smartingly in the fires of abstinence, Hyde would be not even conscious of all that he had lost. Strange as my circumstances were, the terms of this debate are as old and commonplace as man; much the same inducements and alarms cast the die for any tempted and trembling sinner; and it fell out with me, as it falls with so vast a majority of my fellows, that I chose the better part and was found wanting in the strength to keep to it.

> The 'I' at the beginning of this paragraph disassociates itself from both Jekyll and Hyde.
>
> Jekyll is aware of all that Hyde does, Hyde may or may not be aware; but does not care.
>
> Interesting use of father and son relationship to describe Hyde. The device is called antithesis where opposing words or ideas are presented to show contrast. Jekyll cares for Hyde like a father but Hyde does not care for Jekyll in the same way at all.
>
> 'suffer smartingly in the fires of abstinence' – meaning that he could not live a totally good and clean life. he would suffer to do so. Abstain means to stop doing bad things.

Yes, I preferred the elderly and discontented doctor, surrounded by friends and cherishing honest hopes; and bade a resolute farewell to the liberty, the comparative youth, the light step, leaping impulses and secret pleasures, that I had enjoyed in the disguise of Hyde. I made this choice perhaps with some unconscious reservation, for I neither gave up the house in Soho, nor destroyed the clothes of Edward Hyde, which still lay ready in my cabinet. For two months, however, I was true to my determination; for two months, I led a life of such severity as I had never before attained to, and enjoyed the compensations of an approving conscience. But time began at last to obliterate the freshness of my alarm; the praises of conscience began to grow into a thing of course; I began to be tortured with throes and longings, as of Hyde struggling after freedom; and at last, in an hour of moral weakness, I once again compounded and swallowed the transforming draught.

I do not suppose that, when a drunkard reasons with himself upon his vice, he is once out of five hundred times affected by the dangers that he runs through his brutish, physical insensibility; neither had I, long as I had considered my position, made enough allowance for the complete moral insensibility and insensate readiness to evil, which were the leading characters of Edward Hyde. Yet it was by these that I was punished. My devil had been long caged, he came out roaring. I was conscious, even when I took the draught, of a more unbridled, a more furious propensity to ill. It must have been this, I suppose, that stirred in my soul that tempest of impatience with which I listened to the civilities of my unhappy victim; I declare, at least, before God, no man morally sane could have been guilty of that crime upon so pitiful a provocation; and that I struck in no more reasonable spirit than that in which a sick child may break a plaything. But I had voluntarily stripped myself of all those balancing instincts by which even the worst of us continues to walk with some degree of steadiness among temptations; and in my case, to be tempted, however slightly, was to fall.

Instantly the spirit of hell awoke in me and raged. With a transport of glee, I mauled the unresisting body, tasting delight from every blow; and it was not till weariness had begun to succeed, that I was suddenly, in the top fit of my delirium, struck through the heart by a cold thrill of terror. A mist dispersed; I saw my life to be forfeit; and fled from the scene of these excesses, at once glorying and trembling, my lust of evil gratified and stimulated, my love of life screwed to the topmost peg.

> This is Jekyll's remembrance of the brutal murder of Danvers Carew.
>
> Through the terrible violence against the frail old man, Hyde is still aware that this is now murder and can potentially get him hung. Hyde loves his life, and he loves his freedom.
>
> 'mauled' and 'unresisting' – juxtaposition of violence with weak innocence.

I ran to the house in Soho, and (to make assurance doubly sure) destroyed my papers; thence I set out through the lamplit streets, in the same divided ecstasy of mind, gloating on my crime, light-headedly devising others in the future, and yet still hastening and still hearkening in my wake for the steps of the avenger. Hyde had a song upon his lips as he compounded the draught, and as he drank it, pledged the dead man.

> Contrast between Hyde's singing and raising a toast to the dead Sir Danvers, against his reaction as Jekyll, below.

The pangs of transformation had not done tearing him, before Henry Jekyll, with streaming tears of gratitude and remorse, had fallen upon his knees and lifted his clasped hands to God. The veil of self-indulgence was rent from head to foot. I saw my life as a whole: I followed it up from the days of childhood, when I had walked with my father's hand, and through the self-denying toils of my professional life, to arrive again and again, with the same sense of unreality, at the damned horrors of the evening. I could have screamed aloud; I sought with tears and prayers to smother down the crowd of hideous images and sounds with which my memory swarmed against me; and still, between the petitions, the ugly face of my iniquity stared into my soul. As the acuteness of this remorse began to die away, it was succeeded by a sense of joy. The problem of my conduct was solved. Hyde was thenceforth impossible; whether I would or not, I was now confined to the better part of my existence; and O, how I rejoiced to think of it! with what willing humility I embraced anew the restrictions of natural life! with what sincere renunciation I locked the door by which I had so often gone and come, and ground the key under my heel!

> The veil of self-indulgence being 'rent' or ripped is a Biblical allusion. It is in the Gospel of Luke; the veil in a temple was ripped after Jesus died as an act of punishment. Jekyll implies that God is punishing him. Such is the authority of G
>
> The key which he crushes and is later found broken and rusted by Utterson and Poole

The next day, came the news that the murder had been overlooked, that the guilt of Hyde was patent to the world, and that the victim was a man high in public estimation. It was not only a crime, it had been a tragic folly. I think I was glad to know it; I think I was glad to have my better impulses thus buttressed and guarded by the terrors of the scaffold. Jekyll was now my city of refuge; let but Hyde peep out an instant, and the hands of all men would be raised to take and slay him.

I resolved in my future conduct to redeem the past; and I can say with honesty that my resolve was fruitful of some good. You know yourself how earnestly, in the last months of the last year, I laboured to relieve suffering; you know that much was done for others, and that the days passed quietly, almost happily for myself. Nor can I truly say that I wearied of this beneficent and innocent life; I think instead that I daily enjoyed it more completely; but I was still cursed with my duality of purpose; and as the first edge of my penitence wore off, the lower side of me, so indulged, so recently chained down, began to growl for licence. Not that I dreamed of resuscitating Hyde; the bare idea of that would startle me to frenzy: no, it was in my own person that I was once more tempted to trifle with my conscience; and it was as an ordinary secret sinner that I at last fell before the assaults of temptation.

> Jekyll tells how he was extremely good and pious as though that makes up for the brutal murder.
>
> 'scaffold' – where one is hanged.

There comes an end to all things; the most capacious measure is filled at last; and this brief condescension to my evil finally destroyed the balance of my soul. And yet I was not alarmed; the fall seemed natural, like a return to the old days before I had made my discovery. It was a fine, clear, January day, wet under foot where the frost had melted, but cloudless overhead; and the Regent's Park was full of winter chirrupings and sweet with spring odours. I sat in the sun on a bench; the animal within me licking the chops of memory; the spiritual side a little drowsed, promising subsequent penitence, but not yet moved to begin. After all, I reflected, I was like my neighbours; and then I smiled, comparing myself with other men, comparing my active good-will with the lazy cruelty of their neglect.

> Penitence means to be sorry and regretful for having done wrong. Jekyll promises it but does not quite do it. For all that he has done, for all the so called suffering he has endured, it is all not really sincere.

And at the very moment of that vainglorious thought, a qualm came over me, a horrid nausea and the most deadly shuddering. These passed away, and left me faint; and then as in its turn faintness subsided, I began to be aware of a change in the temper of my thoughts, a greater boldness, a contempt of danger, a solution of the bonds of obligation. I looked down; my clothes hung formlessly on my shrunken limbs; the hand that lay on my knee was corded and hairy. I was once more Edward Hyde. A moment before I had been safe of all men's respect, wealthy, beloved—the cloth laying for me in the dining-room at home; and now I was the common quarry of mankind, hunted, houseless, a known murderer, thrall to the gallows.

My reason wavered, but it did not fail me utterly. I have more than once observed that in my second character, my faculties seemed sharpened to a point and my spirits more tensely elastic; thus it came about that, where Jekyll perhaps might have succumbed, Hyde rose to the importance of the moment. My drugs were in one of the presses of my cabinet; how was I to reach them? That was the problem that (crushing my temples in my hands) I set myself to solve. The laboratory door I had closed. If I sought to enter by the house, my own servants would consign me to the gallows. I saw I must employ another hand, and thought of Lanyon. How was he to be reached? how persuaded? Supposing that I escaped capture in the streets, how was I to make my way into his presence? and how should I, an unknown and displeasing visitor, prevail on the famous physician to rifle the study of his colleague, Dr. Jekyll? Then I remembered that of my original character, one part remained to me: I could write my own hand; and once I had conceived that kindling spark, the way that I must follow became lighted up from end to end.

Thereupon, I arranged my clothes as best I could, and summoning a passing hansom, drove to an hotel in Portland Street, the name of which I chanced to remember. At my appearance (which was indeed comical enough, however tragic a fate these garments covered) the driver could not conceal his mirth. I gnashed my teeth upon him with a gust of devilish fury; and the smile withered from his face—happily for him—yet more happily for myself, for in another instant I had certainly dragged him from his perch. At the inn, as I entered, I looked about me with so black a countenance as made the attendants tremble; not a look did they exchange in my presence; but obsequiously took my orders, led me to a private room, and brought me wherewithal to write. Hyde in danger of his life was a creature new to me; shaken with inordinate anger, strung to the pitch of murder, lusting to inflict pain. Yet the creature was astute; mastered his fury with a great effort of the will; composed his two important letters, one to Lanyon and one to Poole; and that he might receive actual evidence of their being posted, sent them out with directions that they should be registered. Thenceforward, he sat all day over the fire in the private room, gnawing his nails; there he dined, sitting alone with his fears, the waiter visibly quailing before his eye; and thence, when the night was fully come, he set forth in the corner of a closed cab, and was driven to and fro about the streets of the city. He, I say—I cannot say, I. That child of Hell had nothing human; nothing lived in him but fear and hatred. And when at last, thinking the driver had begun to grow suspicious, he discharged the cab and ventured on foot, attired in his misfitting clothes, an object marked out for observation, into the midst of the nocturnal passengers, these two base passions raged within him like a tempest. He walked fast, hunted by his fears, chattering to himself, skulking through the less frequented thoroughfares, counting the minutes that still divided him from midnight. Once a woman spoke to him, offering, I think, a box of lights. He smote her in the face, and she fled.

When I came to myself at Lanyon's, the horror of my old friend perhaps affected me somewhat: I do not know; it was at least but a drop in the sea to the abhorrence with which I looked back upon these hours. A change had come over me. It was no longer the fear of the gallows, it was the horror of being Hyde that racked me. I received Lanyon's condemnation partly in a dream; it was partly in a dream that I came home to my own house and got into bed. I slept after the prostration of the day, with a stringent and profound slumber which not even the nightmares that wrung me could avail to break. I awoke in the morning shaken, weakened, but refreshed. I still hated and feared the thought of the brute that slept within me, and I had not of course forgotten the appalling dangers of the day before; but I was once more at home, in my own house and close to my drugs; and gratitude for my escape shone so strong in my soul that it almost rivalled the brightness of hope.

I was stepping leisurely across the court after breakfast, drinking the chill of the air with pleasure, when I was seized again with those indescribable sensations that heralded the change; and I had but the time to gain the shelter of my cabinet, before I was once again raging and freezing with the passions of Hyde. It took on this occasion a double dose to recall me to myself; and alas! six hours after, as I sat looking sadly in the fire, the pangs returned, and the drug had to be re-administered. In short, from that day forth it seemed only by a great effort as of gymnastics, and only under the immediate stimulation of the drug, that I was able to wear the countenance of Jekyll. At all hours of the day and night, I would be taken with the premonitory shudder; above all, if I slept, or even dozed for a moment in my chair, it was always as Hyde that I awakened. Under the strain of this continually impending doom and by the sleeplessness to which I now condemned myself, ay, even beyond what I had thought possible to man, I became, in my own person, a creature eaten up and emptied by fever, languidly weak both in body and mind, and solely occupied by one thought: the horror of my other self. But when I slept, or when the virtue of the medicine wore off, I would leap almost without transition (for the pangs of transformation grew daily less marked) into the possession of a fancy brimming with images of terror, a soul boiling with causeless hatreds, and a body that seemed not strong enough to contain the raging energies of life. The powers of Hyde seemed to have grown with the sickliness of Jekyll. And certainly the hate that now divided them was equal on each side. With Jekyll, it was a thing of vital instinct. He had now seen the full deformity of that creature that shared with him some of the phenomena of consciousness, and was co-heir with him to death: and beyond these links of community, which in themselves made the most poignant part of his distress, he thought of Hyde, for all his energy of life, as of something not only hellish but inorganic. This was the shocking thing; that the slime of the pit seemed to utter cries and voices; that the amorphous dust gesticulated and sinned; that what was dead, and had no shape, should usurp the offices of life. And this again, that that insurgent horror was knit to him closer than a wife, closer than an eye; lay caged in his flesh, where he heard it mutter and felt it struggle to be born; and at every hour of weakness, and in the confidence of slumber, prevailed against him, and deposed him out of life. The hatred of Hyde for Jekyll was of a different order. His terror of the gallows drove him continually to commit temporary suicide, and return to his subordinate station of a part instead of a person; but he loathed the necessity, he loathed the despondency into which Jekyll was now fallen, and he resented the dislike with which he was himself regarded. Hence the ape-like tricks that he would play me, scrawling in my own hand blasphemies on the pages of my books, burning the letters and destroying the portrait of my father; and indeed, had it not been for his fear of death, he would long ago have ruined himself in order to involve me in the ruin. But his love of life is wonderful; I go further: I, who sicken and freeze at the mere thought of him, when I recall the abjection and passion of this attachment, and when I know how he fears my power to cut him off by suicide, I find it in my heart to pity him.

> Jekyll ends up loathing and hating Hyde, contrast this to how he first felt about Hyde. He welcomed him and relished being him. Jekyll however is no longer in control, Hyde is taking over more and more.

It is useless, and the time awfully fails me, to prolong this description; no one has ever suffered such torments, let that suffice; and yet even to these, habit brought—no, not alleviation—but a certain callousness of soul, a certain acquiescence of despair; and my punishment might have gone on for years, but for the last calamity which has now fallen, and which has finally severed me from my own face and nature. My provision of the salt, which had never been renewed since the date of the first experiment, began to run low. I sent out for a fresh supply and mixed the draught; the ebullition followed, and the first change of colour, not the second; I drank it and it was without efficiency. You will learn from Poole how I have had London ransacked; it was in vain; and I am now persuaded that my first supply was impure, and that it was that unknown impurity which lent efficacy to the draught.

> 'efficacy' – the power to produce a desired result.
>
> 'ebullition' – bubbling and boiling.
>
> 'alleviation' – bringing a relief to suffering
>
> 'Acquiescence' – to accept passively, to submit.

About a week has passed, and I am now finishing this statement under the influence of the last of the old powders. This, then, is the last time, short of a miracle, that Henry Jekyll can think his own thoughts or see his own face (now how sadly altered!) in the glass. Nor must I delay too long to bring my writing to an end; for if my narrative has hitherto escaped destruction, it has been by a combination of great prudence and great good luck. Should the throes of change take me in the act of writing it, Hyde will tear it in pieces; but if some time shall have elapsed after I have laid it by, his wonderful selfishness and circumscription to the moment will probably save it once again from the action of his ape-like spite. And indeed the doom that is closing on us both has already changed and crushed him. Half an hour from now, when I shall again and forever reindue that hated personality, I know how I shall sit shuddering and weeping in my chair, or continue, with the most strained and fearstruck ecstasy of listening, to pace up and down this room (my last earthly refuge) and give ear to every sound of menace. Will Hyde die upon the scaffold? or will he find courage to release himself at the last moment? God knows; I am careless; this is my true hour of death, and what is to follow concerns another than myself. Here then, as I lay down the pen and proceed to seal up my confession, I bring the life of that unhappy Henry Jekyll to an end.

It is most likely that Jekyll killed Hyde, that he took the poison at the moment that he changed to Hyde, which was at the same time as Poole breaking down the door.

The impure salt, the chemical which has allowed the transformation, has signalled the end of the novella. The batch that birthed Hyde is no longer available. It was impure and is unlikely to ever be replicated. Coupled with the Hyde transforming now without it, it foreshadows the end.

Jekyll now needs it not to change into Hyde, but to change back into Jekyll. The potion therefore changes from choice to control.

The last paragraph is written in the present tense, bringing a sense of urgency and bringing us closer to the novella, because we feel we are reading it as he is writing it.

# Appendix A: Note Regarding Incorrect Date

The date of Dr Jekyll's letter to Dr Lanyon should be dated the 9th January, not the 10th December, as written in the text.

*The Norton Anthology of English Literature* explains the error thus:

> Stevenson's own error; the first sentence of 'Dr. Lanyon's Narrative' makes it clear that the letter should be dated '9th January.' Literary critic Richard Dury attributes the slip to the following circumstances: Stevenson had originally wanted to publish his story in time for the Christmas market and align Lanyon's witnessing of Hyde's transformation with December, a time for mysterious events. Later he forgot to change the detail. (794n1)

# Appendix B: Works Cited

*Stevenson, Robert Louis. Strange Case of Dr. Jekyll and Mr. Hyde. 1886.*

*The Norton Anthology of British Literature: The Victorian Age. 10th ed. Stephen Greenblatt, General Editor; Catherine Robson, Volume Editor. W.W. Norton, 2018. pp. 767-809.*

# Appendix C: The Home of Jekyll/Hyde

In *The Strange Case of Dr Jekyll and Mr Hyde*, the address of the home of Dr Henry Jekyll (and his alter-ego Mr Edward Hyde) is not specified, although Mr Hyde had procured rooms in Soho, which at the time was a very seedy and poor part of London.

Dr Jekyll is said to have bought his property from the heirs of a "celebrated surgeon". Like Dr Jekyll, the house has two characters and features a "blistered and distained" rear entrance, as used by Mr Hyde.

In a BBC Scotland documentary broadcast several years ago, author Ian Rankin identified the house in which Jekyll and Hyde lived as being based on that which pioneering Scottish surgeon and anatomist John Hunter (1728-1793) lived in on the east side of Leicester Square.

Hunter leased both the property at 28 Leicester Square (the present number 28 – the ground floor of which is a pub – is pictured) and another behind it (it fronted onto what was then Castle Street) in the 1780s. He then spent a good deal of money joining the two properties together, creating a complex of rooms which included space for his thousands of specimens (now in the Hunterian Museum) as well as an anatomy theatre. It was at the rear Castle Street entrance that he apparently received human cadavers, brought by so-called "resurrection men" for dissection.

Hunter dissected over 2000 human bodies, supplied by grave robbers. This was extremely lucrative work at the time. Burke and Hare were famous body snatchers operating in Edinburgh. So lucrative was the work that when there were no fresh bodies to be dug up, they turned to murder.

The dualistic nature of the property fits with that of Jekyll and Hyde and while Leicester Square isn't usually considered part of Soho, it is close by.

"In the book, Stevenson gives a detailed description of the layout of Dr Jekyll's home," Rankin said in the documentary. "It is identical to John Hunter's."

He added that, despite Hunter's "fame and respectability" – he was appointed Surgeon Extraordinary to King George III and was one of London's most sought-after doctors, "Hunter still demanded a constant supply of cadavers for his growing anatomy collection and teaching".

"Naturally Hunter's new home, in Leicester Square, was purpose-built for a surgeon's double life." Or for the respectable Dr Jekyll and the brutish Mr Hyde.

Interestingly, the previous owner of Dr Jekyll's home us said to have been a Dr Denman – there was a Dr Thomas Denman, a pioneering obstetrician, who was a contemporary of John Hunter.

The Leicester Square property later became the site of the Royal Panopticon of Science and Art.

*Number 28 Leicester Square as it is today*

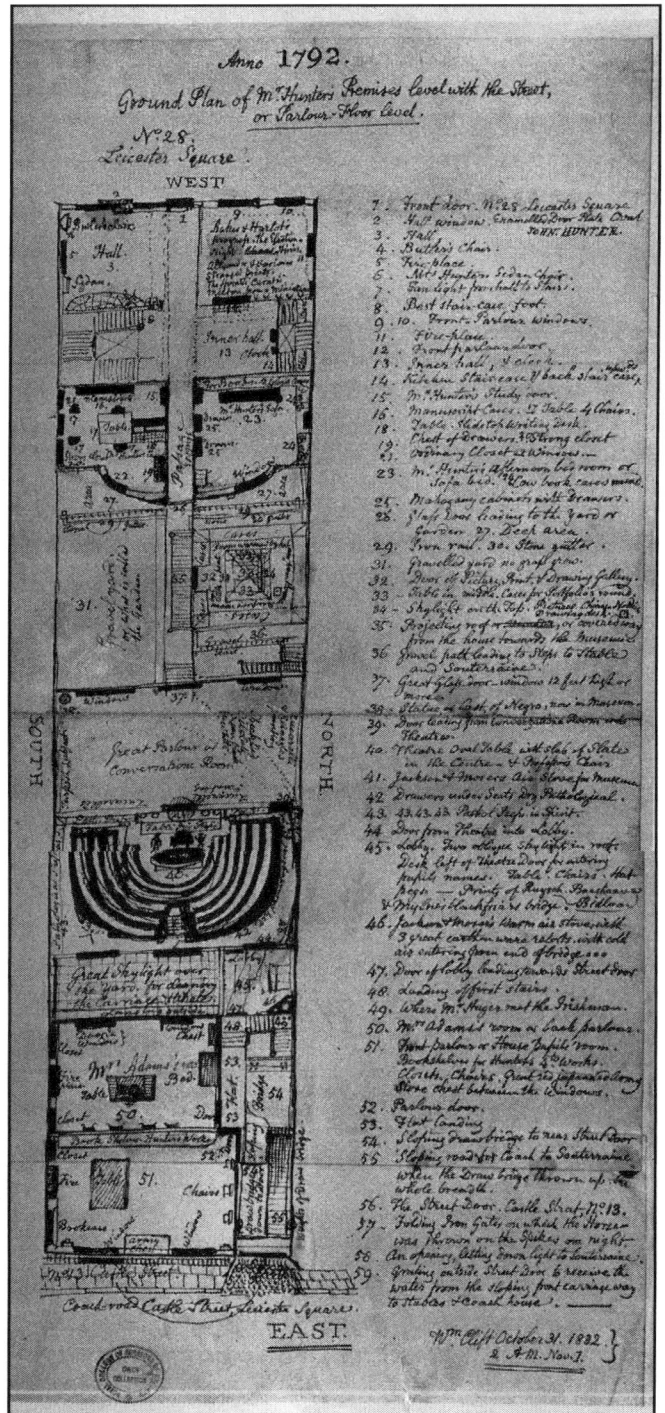

*A ground floor plan of John Hunter's residence made in 1792 (drawn in 1832)*

# Appendix D: Glossary

While some words have been defined in the annotated play, others are detailed below.

Connotations reveal clear connections to the primary themes of duality, mystery, evil and reputation, as well as anything to do with power and control, the relationship between weakness and strength, good and evil.

Evil manifests itself in forms of violence, threat and menace, while good manifests itself as weak, frail, delicate, with the two locked in seeking control, the one over the other.

Good and Evil are concepts that can be polarized by Religiosity, in terms of God and the Devil. However, to polarize these concepts under secularism (meaning non-religious aspects), we thus use the context as presented by Darwin and Freud.

Good and evil are definable when placed within the parameters of religion. God and His teachings lay down what is good and what is evil. God becomes the epitome of what we deem as being good, and the Devil becomes polarised as all that is evil. Therefore, for those readers who are religious, good and evil can be understood and defined through this concept.

However, things become complicated for those readers who are not of the faith. For a Secular readership, meaning a non-religious/atheist readership, RLS has presented good and evil through other means.

## Chapter 1

| | |
|---|---|
| **aptness** | rightness, appropriateness |
| **austere** | strict, unsmiling (repression) |
| **countenance** | face, outward look, exterior (reputation) |
| **demeanour** | behaviour, appearance (reputation) |
| **modest** | reserved, discreet (repression, reputation) |
| **proprieties** | correct, respectable (reputation) |
| **reprove** | criticize, tell off (solidarity) |
| **sordid** | disreputable, dirty, immoral (evil) |

## Chapter 2

| | |
|---|---|
| **M.D.** | Doctor of Medicine |
| **D.C.L.** | Doctor of Civil Law, |
| **L.L.D.** | Doctor of Laws, |
| **F.R.S.** | Fellow of the Royal Society. |
| **bachelor** | unmarried man, never been married |
| **balderdash** | nonsense |
| **blackguardly** | scoundrel, villain, evil |

*Note: In the 19th century, the first two of these were degrees earned at a medical school and the second two were professional career awards.*

| | |
|---|---|
| **brandishing** | wielding, displaying (reputation) |
| **bond** | relationship, friendship (solidarity) |
| **bondage** | slavery, oppression, repression (duality) |
| **concourse** | open space, square |
| **condoned** | overlook, excuse, ignore (solidarity) |
| **conflagration** | fire, inferno |
| **contrived** | plan, scheme, plot (power and control, duality) |
| **conveyancing** | the act of transferring property from one person to another (duality) |
| **echo** | a duplicate, a copy (duality) |
| **endorsed** | permitted, allowed (power and control-duality) |
| **enslaved** | caged, made a slave of (duality) |
| **estranged** | divided, separated (duality) |
| **fronted** | At the front (reputation) |
| **haggard** | faded, tired |
| **hitherto** | until now |
| **indignation** | anger, offence, connotations of arrogance (power and control) |
| **iniquity** | evil, immorality, vice |
| **inordinate** | excessive, extravagant, extra |
| **insensate** | unconscious, heartless, having no senses |
| **insubstantial** | flimsy, thin, light (mystery) |
| **lurid** | loud, shocking, vivid |
| **mangled** | crushed, battered, mauled, disfigured (evil) |
| **napery** | table linen (cover-reputation) |
| **obnoxious** | repulsive, loathsome, abhorrent (evil) |
| **obscure** | vague, unclear, opaque (mystery) |
| **odious** | abhorrent, disgusting, repellent, abominable (evil) |
| **presentment** | presentation, outwardly (reputation) |
| **prevision** | predicting a future event, foresight (supernatural) |
| **protégé** | dependant (duality) |
| **reflection** | likeness, image (duality) |
| **superstitious** | having or showing a belief in supernatural influences, a belief that is not based on human reason or scientific knowledge, but is connected with old ideas about magic, etc. (opposite of reason, facts and logic); secular polarisation of good v evil |
| **troglodytic** | caveman, primal, (duality) |

## Chapter 3

| | |
|---|---|
| **abominable** | horrible, monstrous, dreadful, fearful (evil) |
| **cheval glass** | tall, full-length mirror that flips over |
| **cupola** | glass dome in ceiling (mystery) |
| **elicited** | provoked, caused |
| **incoherency** | confusion, disjointed (mystery) |
| **irrepressible** | uncontrollable, wild, wilful |
| **sedulously** | carefully, painstakingly |
| **unobtrusive** | bland, modest, shy, inconspicuous (hypocrisy of MCM) |

## Chapter 4

| | |
|---|---|
| **disposition** | nature, character, temperament |
| **fugitive** | outlaw, criminal, escapee (duality) |
| **insensate** | inert, unconscious |
| **quailed** | trembled, show fear, cowered |

## Chapter 5

| | |
|---|---|
| **anatomical** | of the body |
| **cupola** | dome, roof (mystery) |
| **gaunt** | haggard, emaciated, ill |
| **heirs** | successors, inheritors (duality) |
| **oration** | speech, lecture |
| **quaint** | pretty in an old-fashioned way |
| **qualm** | doubt, fear, foreboding |
| **ruminated** | contemplated, thought about |

## Chapter 6

| | |
|---|---|
| **callous** | cold, heartless |
| **condemned** | doomed, found guilty |
| **consciousness** | awareness, realisation |
| **disreputable** | scandalous, disgraceful (reputation) |
| **sinister** | menacing, ominous, evil |
| **stringent** | severe, strict |
| **unmanning** | to remove manliness from, to unnerve, crush |

# Chapter 7

| | |
|---|---|
| **abject** | miserable, gloomy, dismal (weakness) |
| **disconsolate** | sad, dejected (weakness) |
| **thoroughfare** | access, way (knowledge) |

# Chapter 8

| | |
|---|---|
| **ails** | troubles, distress |
| **blasphemies** | doing things against God |
| **commend** | praise, applaud |
| **diaphanous** | transparent, gauzy, filmy, (mystery and clarity) |
| **disinterred** | exposed, revealed, unveiled (mystery) |
| **exorbitant** | excessive |
| **flecked** | speckled, splashed, marked (violence) |
| **hoarsely** | rasping, husky (animalistic; secular depiction of evil) |
| **lamentation** | crying, weeping (weakness) |
| **malefactor** | criminal, offender |
| **peril** | danger |
| **pious** | devout, religious (hypocrisy) |
| **sedulous** | zealous, diligent |
| **solemnly** | seriously |

# Chapter 9

| | |
|---|---|
| **accoutrement** | accessory, equipment |
| **acuteness** | sharpness, perceptiveness |
| **cerebral** | intellectual, rational |
| **convulsive** | jerky, violent, uncontrollable |
| **crystalline** | like crystal, sparkling |
| **debility** | weakness, frailty |
| **dispensing** | supply, provision |
| **ebullition** | explosion, fizzing, outburst connotes violence |
| **enigmas** | puzzles (mystery) |
| **gloomy** | unhappy, sad, dark, depressing |
| **idiosyncratic** | characteristic, individual |

| **impediment** | something that holds you back, a hindrance, obstacle |
|---|---|
| **incipient** | emerging, embryonic, early, primal |
| **metamorphoses** | transformation, mutation, transformation, transfiguration |
| **misbegotten** | bad, ill-conceived, improper |
| **penitence** | regret, sorrow, contrition, remorse |
| **phial** | ampoule, test tube |
| **portico** | entry, doorway |
| **province** | area, region |
| **rigour** | severity, harsh |
| **subjective** | personal, individual |
| **transcendental** | mystical, heavenly, supernatural, divine |
| **turpitude** | immorality, wickedness, depravity (evil) |
| **volatile** | unstable, explosive, unpredictable |

# Chapter 10

| **abhorrence** | hatred, repulsion, rejection |
|---|---|
| **abjection** | misery, despair, low (weakness) |
| **abstinence** | self-denial, restraint (repression) |
| **acquiescence** | consent, agreement, submission (weakness) |
| **astute** | wise, intelligent |
| **avail** | benefit, gain |
| **bestial avidity** | beast like greed) |
| **buttress** | support, reinforce |
| **callousness** | cruel, cold hearted (evil) |
| **civilities** | courtesies, respects, giving deference and respect to |
| **commingled** | blend, fuse, merge |
| **compounded** | combined |
| **condemnation** | disapproval, criticism |
| **condescension** | arrogance, disdain |
| **denizens** | residents, inhabitants |
| **depravity** | immorality, evil, vice, wickedness |
| **despondency** | sadness, hopelessness |
| **dissociated** | detached, separated, disconnected |

| | |
|---|---|
| **dissolution** | terminating, ending, cessation |
| **duality** | two sides, two aspects, good v evil, weak v strong |
| **duplicity** | deceit, treachery, dishonesty (secular presentation of evil) |
| **earnest** | serious, solemn, sober |
| **endowed** | gifted, given |
| **extraneous** | unnecessary, non-essential, extra |
| **exultation** | happiness, triumph |
| **forfeited** | lost, surrendered, sacrificed (duality) |
| **genial** | friendly, hospitable |
| **hearkening** | pay attention listen to, give consideration to |
| **humility** | self-effaced, humble, shy |
| **hypocrite** | fraud, double-dealer, dissembler, pretender |
| **impenetrable** | impossible to pass through or enter, impassable, thick, dark, murky |
| **imperious** | domineering, arrogant, superior |
| **incongruous** | strange, out of place, odd |
| **inducements** | incentive, enticement |
| **inexplicable** | mysterious, perplexing (mystery) |
| **infallible** | perfect, unflawed |
| **infallibly** | perfectly, faultlessly |
| **insensibility** | cruel, unfeeling, callous |
| **insurgent** | rebel, uprising, revolution (rising of lower classes) |
| **inveterately** | hardened, chronic, ingrained, incurable, deep-rooted |
| **irrevocably** | irreversibly, permanently |
| **kindling** | burning, igniting |
| **languidly** | lazily, lethargically |
| **multifarious** | diverse, mixed, various |
| **mystic** | magic |
| **obligation** | responsibility, duty |
| **obsequiously** | sycophantic, submissive |
| **pecuniary** | monetary |
| **penitence** | shame, repentance, atonement, contrition |
| **perennia** | recurring, persistent, perpetual |
| **potently** | powerfully |

| | |
|---|---|
| **premonitory** | forewarning, omen, sign |
| **primitive** | primal, prehistoric |
| **profound** | deep, intense, philosophical |
| **propensity** | tendency, inclination |
| **reconcile** | reunite, merge, bring together |
| **renunciation** | rejection, refute, abandonment, disavowal |
| **repugnance** | disgust, dislike, hate |
| **robust** | full-bodied, healthy, strong, tough |
| **skulking** | lurk, creep |
| **slavery** | ownership of a person by another. |
| **smote** | hit, struck |
| **stature** | physique, reputation |
| **succumbed** | yielded, given in, died |
| **tabernacle** | temple (secular meaning for body) |
| **tempest** | storm |
| **transcendental** | mystical, supernatural, divine, heavenly |
| **transience** | fleeting, impermanence, ephemeral (secular meaning for soul) |
| **unbridled** | unrestrained, rampant, uncontrolled |
| **unscrupulous** | immoral, corrupt (secular meaning for evil) |
| **vainglorious** | arrogant, big-headed, narcissistic |
| **vestment** | garment, clothing (secular meaning for body; hide; reputation; duality) |
| **vicarious** | remote, indirect |
| **vigilance** | watchfulness, caution |

| | |
|---|---|
| **amorphous dust gesticulated and sinned** | amorphous means having no clear shape or definition. Dust means dry, fine powder, dust, connoting human body; gesticulated means to make the sign of the cross; sin connotes to commit evil acts as a Christian term. |
| **impenetrable mantle** | a layer that cannot be broken (Hyde) |
| **stamping efficacy** | imprinting; ability – Jekyll means he had transferred 'control stamping efficacy' to the evil side of his nature. (duality) |
| **thrall to the gallows** | bondage, slave to the gallows |

Printed in Great Britain
by Amazon